The Church Treasurer's Handbook

The Church Treasurer's Handbook

Robert Leach, FCCA ACA

CANTERBURY
PRESS
Norwich

First published in 2005 by Canterbury Press Norwich
Canterbury Press is an imprint of
Hymns Ancient & Modern Limited (a registered charity)
13a Hellesdon Park Road, Norwich, NR6 5DR

www.canterburypress.co.uk

New edition 2012

British Library Cataloguing in Publication data
A catalogue record for this book is available
from the British Library

ISBN 978-1-84825-019-2

Typeset by Regent Typesetting, London
Printed and bound by
CPI Group (UK) Ltd, Croydon, CR0 4YY

Contents

I

Introduction

Role of treasurer

The treasurer is the church's trusted officer who looks after its funds for the common good.

Sometimes churches tend to see such administrative functions as being lesser than other forms of ministry, such as preaching or counselling. It is unfortunate that the disciples' treasurer was Judas Iscariot. However, scripture is quite clear that administration is one of the gifts of the Spirit (Romans 12.7). The church treasurer offers time and talents as an act of stewardship, which should bring its own blessings and joys. Being church treasurer is not just a valuable ministry, it is an essential ministry.

Looking after the church's money is similar to looking after your own funds, or looking after the funds of a commercial business, but with one significant difference. Generally you or a business are free to do what you wish with your funds; a church or charity usually has *restricted* funds the purpose of which is confined to a stated aim (see page 12). Most of the special accounting provisions for churches and charities are designed to deal with restricted funds.

Qualities of treasurer

The treasurer need not be qualified as an accountant, but must be:

- conscientious
- organized
- of the highest integrity.

If you doubt whether you meet the last of these conditions, you probably do.

The minister, church council and congregation must all have confidence in the treasurer. The treasurer must be discrete and able to keep confidences (see page 205).

Almost all of us administer our own finances. Being a treasurer largely involves the same skills most of us already have. The additional skills needed are easily learned, and simply formalize procedures we probably all follow already.

Most congregations include accountants. However, many accountants in the church may be unwilling to be treasurer for proper reasons. The accountant may feel that he needs a break from his work when at church, he may believe that God is calling him to a different ministry, or he may feel constrained by professional rules. Such an unwillingness should be accepted by the church with good grace. However, such accountants may be willing to help the treasurer if he encounters a particular problem.

Trusting the treasurer

The treasurer's work is checked by an auditor or examiner (see page 195). Various church officers may be assumed to have rights of inspection. In addition, the treasurer will be held to account by the church council and annual general meeting (or equivalents). Sometimes the treasurer may feel that he is not trusted: that is rarely the case.

If the church authorities do cease to trust you, they should not allow you to continue as treasurer. Being audited, monitored and held to account is a routine part of the treasurer's job. In most cases that is how it should be seen. Sometimes a minister or trustee may be insecure or lacking in understanding, which is why he persists in asking questions. Most other officers will have considerably less understanding of the finances than yourself. Accept all questions and requests for checking with good grace.

Sadly, there have been a few cases when treasurers have abused their position by stealing church funds. There have been many more instances where honest treasurers have got into a muddle. Auditing, monitoring and reporting should be seen as supporting the treasurer, not undermining him.

Introduction

Routine of treasurer

Probably the most important discipline for a treasurer is to be organized. Pieces of paper, odd amounts of cash and sundry requests can come at you from all directions at all times. You must have a system to ensure that none go astray and that you know what every item means.

A good system is that the treasurer has an in-tray or 'pigeon hole' or similar in the church from which all documents are collected once a week. This avoids losing a scrap of paper which you absent-mindedly thrust in a pocket while thinking of something else.

A simple system is to have weekly, monthly and annual routines, and to set aside time for these routines. You may set aside an hour or so every Sunday afternoon for the weekly routine, for example. It is advisable to have an 'in-tray' at home so all the sundry pieces of paper which come to you are immediately put where you can easily find them. You can waste many frustrating hours searching for a scrap of paper that Mrs Jones gave you after a church service. If told things, write them down as soon as possible, but discourage verbal communications.

Almost certainly, the treasurer will need to spend some time every week on his duties. This is not a task which can be done in a few days before the annual report.

The *weekly* routine may include:

- banking the week's collections
- entering income and expenditure into the records
- paying bills.

The *monthly* routine may include:

- reconciling the bank statement to the cash book
- running the payroll.

The *annual* routine may include:

- preparing the annual accounts
- submitting the year-end tax return
- submitting an annual return to a central church authority
- writing an annual report for church members.

3

Purpose of treasurer

A church prepares accounts so that it knows how much:

- income it has received
- expenditure it has incurred
- money it has at the year end.

If in doubt on how to proceed on any issue, consider which way best meets those objectives.

As with all jobs, there are laws and other rules which must be followed. However, the task is not onerous for a person with the appropriate aptitude and willingness. Most rules can be understood more clearly if you consider why they were made.

A treasurer should not be paid for his work. This is specifically banned in the Church of England and many other denominations. The treasurer should usually be a member of the church council and any standing committee. The treasurer must have easy access to the minister and to all other leaders in the church.

In some cases, it may be appropriate for the church to engage the services of a paid **professional accountant**. Such examples could be to fight a tax appeal, negotiate a debt or oversee a major contract. This is quite proper, and such an accountant is not the church treasurer but someone answerable to the treasurer.

It is good practice for every church to appoint an **assistant treasurer** who can deputize in the treasurer's absence. It is also good practice for at least two people to be aware of all financial matters connected with the church.

In addition to the treasurer, every church should have a separate person as auditor or examiner.

Duties of treasurer

The duties of a treasurer include:

- recording income and expenditure of the church
- looking after the funds
- reporting the financial position.

Income and expenditure are reported for an **accounting period**, which is usually a year to an accounting date. The only exceptions are in the first and last years of the church's existence, and if the church should change its accounting date for any reason.

The Church of England and most other denominations require that the accounts are prepared for the calendar year, that is the period from 1 January to 31 December. Other bodies may prepare accounts for different financial years. For example, many companies prepare accounts for years from 1 April to 31 March.

Depending on the church, the treasurer may have other duties, possibly shared with other officers. Such duties may include:

- counting the collection
- banking the collection
- paying staff
- recording pledged giving
- reclaiming tax on giving
- arranging insurance cover
- administering trust funds
- preparing budgets and forecasts
- running a stewardship campaign
- keeping an assets register.

Some churches prefer to give some of these tasks to other people. It is common for stewardship and pledged giving to be administered by separate officers, and for churchwardens (or their equivalent) to keep the assets register. The treasurer should be clear at the outset, exactly what his duties are. All of the above are covered in this book.

Support

The treasurer, like all church officers, should have access to training and support. Increasingly, dioceses and other bodies are now offering training in both basic disciplines of being a church treasurer and in specific topics such as new legislation as it arises.

It is useful to know another experienced church treasurer who can help with sudden problems. Often a diocese or other central body will have someone who can help.

You can keep up to date in matters concerning church treasurers by joining the Association of Church Accountants and Treasurers (ACAT).

2

Record Keeping

BASIC PRINCIPLES

Objectives

Record keeping must be:

- simple
- understandable
- accurate
- timely
- accessible.

An efficient system of record keeping is at the heart of being an effective treasurer. The exact form will depend on the size of the church, the circumstances in which you work, the exact scope of the treasurer's job, and your own preferences. But remember that the system works for you; you do not work for the system.

The treasurer can decide whether to use a manual or computer system. The principles are the same. Computer systems simply mechanize the manual processes. They even use similar terms such as 'folders', 'documents' and 'cut and paste'.

It is good practice for the treasurer to put all financial transactions through a bank account. Avoid transactions being paid in cash from the collection as this makes the disciplines and audit of the accounts difficult. If ready cash is needed by the church, operate a petty cash system where funds are drawn from the bank and properly controlled (see page 37). In churches where casual financial arrangements exist, such disciplines may not be welcome; they soon will after you and the auditor have included a note in the annual accounts that they cannot be sure these accounts are reliable because of a lack of financial control!

Simple records

A common failing of treasurers is to set up a complicated system capable of producing a vast amount of analysis which is not needed.

The function of the treasurer is to record income and expenditure, and analyse each under main categories. It is unlikely that a church will need more than ten main categories of income and fifteen categories of expenditure.

A typical list of income and expenditure categories is given in Figure 1.

Figure 1: Typical income and expenditure categories in church accounts

Income	Expenditure
Pledged giving	Parish share (or any payment to central body)
Tax recovered	
Loose collections	Maintenance of building
Fees for weddings, etc.	Office expenses
Investment income	Maintaining minister's home
Hiring of hall	Worship expenses
Magazine sales	Sunday school
Bookstall sales	Music
Refreshment sales	Youth work
Fund-raising activities	Donations to charities
Grants and legacies	Church staff
Transfers from accounts	Stationery and telephone
Other	Electricity and gas
	Hall-hiring expenses
	Magazine expenses
	Refreshment expenses
	Transfers to accounts
	Other

Each church probably may have at least one other item of income and expenditure which is relevant. A city church may receive significant income from letting out its car park during the week. A church in a tough area may spend significant sums on security. If there is a significant item of income and expenditure specific to your church, there should be a category for that. However, still keep the number of categories of each to around ten to fifteen.

Anglican churches may wish to have separate categories for parochial fees. These are paid in respect of weddings and funerals at a statutory rate and passed to the diocese. In practice, churches often charge a single fee, particularly for weddings, which includes the statutory fees along with additional fees such as for flowers, music, orders of service and other church facilities. Such fees should be apportioned between the various categories.

Another category which may be useful is that of Agency. This relates to situations where the church receives money to pass on to someone else. This includes parochial fees payable to the diocese, donations for specific charities, and payments earmarked for particular church officers. An Agency category may be created in both income and expenditure. At the end of the year, the balance on the Agency category should be zero as all payments received for payment to someone else should have been paid.

It is good practice for columns to be added to the same categories of income and expenditure on each page. Although not essential, this is good practice as it reduces the likelihood of mistakes and makes the books simpler to understand. The exact order of the categories is purely a matter for the convenience and preference of the treasurer.

Too much analysis is counter-productive. Normally, a church needs to know how much it costs to maintain its building. It does not need separate figures for cutting the grass, polishing the floor, cleaning the windows, mending pews and so on. Similarly, a church does not need to know separate figures for the vicarage water rates and altar candles. Even the telephone bill need not be disclosed separately, but can be included with stationery or office expenses. If the minister or church council wishes to know such information, it is better to produce it as a separate exercise on request, than to produce vast amounts of analysis on the off-chance that someone may want it.

All accounts are intended to paint a picture. A good picture focuses the eye on what is important, and does not distract the eye with irrelevant detail. If you do believe that some detail is needed, still prepare the simple accounts which give the overall picture, and then cross-reference the relevant part of the accounts to a separate statement giving the details.

There is always an 'Other' or 'Sundry' category for both income and expenditure for those items which do not fit into any other category, such as insurance claims, legal action and similar unusual items. Provided the total for such items is neither large nor significant in any other way, this is perfectly proper.

The process of *how* to analyse expenditure is explained on page 32.

Remember that the law and accounting standards only state the *minimum* information you must disclose. You are always at liberty to disclose more information if you believe it is necessary to help understand the accounts. In practice, it can be better to have the information available but still to produce just simple accounts.

Understandable records

It must be possible for another treasurer or an accountant to look at the records at any stage of preparation, and understand them. There must never be a need for a treasurer to explain how the records are kept: it must be obvious.

If a treasurer has to explain the accounting records to an accountant or auditor, the treasurer is not keeping proper records. It is convenient and usual for the treasurer to give an overview explanation to the auditor or examiner, but it must never be an *essential* part of understanding the records.

The basic requirements of understandable accounts are:

- every page and every document has a heading, such as 'Deposit account, income April 2012'
- all items are written neatly
- there are no deletions or amendments which make it unclear what the figure is
- no cryptic abbreviations are used (the auditor may not know that PYG is the parish youth group)
- there is a proper audit trail (see page 17).

Accurate records

It is obvious that records have no purpose unless accurate. However, that does not necessitate spurious accuracy, particularly with regard to rounding and estimating.

For rounding, the general rule is:

- keep records to the nearest penny
- publish accounts to the nearest pound.

Nothing is gained by reporting that the annual income was £147,692.14 rather than £147,692. This is an example of unnecessary detail crowding the true picture.

Sometimes it may be necessary to estimate an amount. The church may have agreed some building work and not yet know the full cost, or be in dispute about the cost. In such cases, the treasurer must:

- estimate a reasonable figure, erring on the side of caution
- state in the accounts that it is an estimate.

Timely records

Financial records must be kept up to date, in that all income and expenditure should be entered in a cash book or computer equivalent within a reasonable time. For income, that is likely to be no more than a day or two. For expenditure, provided details are noted on a cheque stub, it is probably sufficient that expenditure is written up once a month.

A treasurer usually needs to do some work at least once a week. Many treasurers find it convenient to set aside a regular time each week for this. A treasurer should not start work in a blaze of enthusiasm and then let things slip once the enthusiasm has waned.

Accessible records

Records must be accessible both to the treasurer and to anyone else who is legitimately entitled to see them. This always includes the minister, and usually it will include the churchwardens, trustees or equivalent. The auditor or examiner has the right to see such records whenever he wishes; the audit is not necessarily restricted to an audit period. Such people must know where the accounts are kept.

There is no objection to keeping the accounts at the treasurer's home rather than on church premises, provided the exact location is known to at least two other people, such as an assistant treasurer and the auditor (or examiner).

The right to inspect the accounts does not mean that the auditor can knock on your door and demand immediate sight of the records in the middle of a dinner party. It does mean that such a person may ask to see the records at a convenient time and place at no more than a few days' notice.

If you go away on holiday or for any other reason, the records should be temporarily transferred to another location and arrangements made for day-to-day transactions to continue and be properly recorded.

Types of funds

A treasurer must understand that the church may hold up to four types of funds:

1 endowment funds
2 restricted funds
3 designated funds
4 unrestricted funds

Endowment funds

These are often funds where only the interest may be spent. Technically, such funds are called **capital endowment funds** or **permanent endowments**. For example, an individual donates £100,000 which is invested at (say) 5% a year providing an indefinite income of £5,000 a year for a specific purpose. The £100,000 is the capital and £5,000 is the interest. Any expenses of administering an endowment fund should be charged to that fund and not to unrestricted funds.

In accounting, the capital of the endowment does not appear in the church accounts at all, but in a separate note to the accounts. The interest is included as income for the appropriate type of fund. In such a case, both the £100,000 capital and £5,000 a year interest will lose their value as the years pass. This is known as **withering on the vine**. While a few per cent each year may not seem much, the effect over a long period is immense. Inflation led to a sixty-six-fold increase in prices during the twentieth century, and a thirty-fold increase since 1945. This means that £100,000 to-day is worth about £1,500 from 100 years ago. If the twenty-first century has similar inflation to the twentieth, £100,000 and £5,000 today will be worth about £1,500 and £75 in a hundred years' time. How to deal with funds which have become small during the passing of years is addressed on page 174.

There is also a rare creature, the **expendable endowment fund**, where the church is allowed to spend the capital as well as the interest. In such a case, the capital (or so much of it as may be spent) is included with the appropriate restricted, designated or unrestricted fund.

An endowment fund may hold assets in addition to funds. Someone may leave a house on the basis that the church may spend the rent generated, for example. If the asset is sold, the proceeds must be treated as part of the same endowment fund.

Restricted funds

These are when the church is not allowed to do what it wishes and may only use them for a specific purpose, such as to maintain the buildings or to replace the church hall one day. Restricted funds commonly arise from legacies where the deceased stated the restriction. This is legally binding on the church.

The restriction is imposed either by the donor or by the church. A donor may leave money on condition that it is used to maintain the church building, or the bells, or whatever. Alternatively the church may have launched an appeal for a specific purpose, such as to replace the roof or build an extension. The money collected for such a specific appeal must be used only for that purpose.

For this reason, it is advisable to say at the outset what the church authorities intend to do with any surplus. The restriction then only applies until the original objective has been satisfied. If a church appeals for funds to replace the roof, raises £120,000 but only needs £100,000, a statement at the outset that any excess funds will be held to maintain the church fabric generally will allow that £20,000 excess to be transferred to a fabric fund where it could be used to repair the floor or walls the following year. If it did not make such a statement at the outset, the £20,000 would have to be held in a roof fund where it may not be needed for thirty years while the church is desperate for funds for other purposes.

Another issue is what the church will do if it raises insufficient funds. A church may always use unrestricted funds to meet an objective of a restricted fund, provided it has or can generate sufficient unrestricted funds. Otherwise it is advisable to say at the outset that insufficient restricted funds will be used for another but related purpose.

The treasurer must know exactly what the restrictions are for each fund. A restricted fund to replace the church hall cannot be used to maintain the existing hall. Conversely, if the church incurs expenditure within the scope of a restricted fund, the treasurer should use the restricted fund rather than unrestricted funds.

Sometimes there may be a **special trust** which is defined in Charities Act 1993 s.97 as 'property which is held and administered by or on behalf of a charity for any special purposes of the charity, and is so held and administered on separate trusts relating only to that property'. Such funds are treated as a restricted fund of the church.

In practice, the only advantage of a restricted fund is that people tend to give more generously when a purpose is specifically identified.

It should be noted that a church is not obliged to accept any donation, and may wish to refuse if the restrictions are unreasonable, particularly if the amount is small.

Designated funds

These are when the church itself has set aside some of its money for a specific purpose. For example, the church may realize that it will need £250,000 to replace its church hall in ten years' time, so it resolves to set aside £25,000 a year to pay for this. This is not a restricted fund as the church authority can at any time decide to reverse its decision and spend the sum as it wishes. Neither is this an unrestricted fund, as the church does not wish to spend this sum on anything else.

A designated fund must be for a specific purpose and must be approved by the church council, diaconate, trustees or similar body. A designated fund must not be created by the treasurer acting alone. Sometimes treasurers have created designated funds to 'squirrel' away surpluses to make the church accounts look less prosperous.

Rather than produce accounts showing that the church made a surplus of £21,467 one year, the treasurer may be tempted to transfer £20,000 to a designated fund, perhaps for building maintenance, and show a surplus of just £1,467. Sometimes this can be done to create a sense of the church 'just about paying its way' as an incentive for people to keep giving, and to prevent church members coming up with unwelcome ideas on how to spend this surplus. While understandable, this is a form of deception on the church members, even if you correctly report the transactions. By the time the annual accounts are prepared, the church authorities should have decided what to do with any surplus, and that should be included in the treasurer's report.

Unrestricted funds

These are when the church is free to do what it wishes with the money. For most churches, most of the funds should be unrestricted. This is what you use to pay the routine bills. Any fund which is not an endowment, designated or restricted comes within the scope of unrestricted funds.

It is not necessary for these funds to be kept in separate bank accounts, though an endowment fund will often be in a separate investment account anyway. It is possible for restricted and designated funds with any surplus unrestricted funds to be kept in a deposit account while unrestricted funds are kept in a current account on which the day-to-day cheques are drawn.

Old funds

Before 1993, there was no specific requirement in the Charities Act to separate restricted and unrestricted funds in the same way (though trust law has always required some separation of different funds), so some old funds may contain a mixture. A common example is a fabric fund which may contain restricted funds from specific appeals and designated funds allocated by the church council. The basis of how those funds arose may have been lost.

Where an old fund is mixed, the charity should go back as far as it can in its records. Since 1960, charities have been obliged to keep records for the previous six years, though many churches keep accounts indefinitely as part of their history.

THE RECORDS

The choice

Having understood the objectives, the treasurer should decide what form the records should take. The choice is between bound books and a computer system. Note that looseleaf files are generally not acceptable. Records must be seen to be timely and unfalsified. This is much more difficult for looseleaf records than for a bound book.

Each has advantages and disadvantages. Computer system have the advantage that copies are easily made, and calculations and reconciliations are easily prepared. Against that, bound books have the advantage that you do not need a computer or print-out to read them, and they are simpler to keep up to date.

Computer systems tend to copy the disciplines of manual accounting systems. For this reason, we consider the requirements of record keeping in terms of manual records written in ink on the pages of a book, and then separately consider the additional factors for computer records.

Basic disciplines in handwritten accounts

1. *All entries must be made in permanent ink*

It is never acceptable for entries in accounting records to be in pencil or some other erasable form. Entries may be made in fountain pen, ballpoint pen, rollerball pens or with any other permanent writing implement.

2. *All entries must be legible*

There must never be any doubt as to what the entry says. This usually means writing numbers more slowly and carefully than normal. It is easy for 1 and 7, and for 0 and 6 to look similar when written quickly.

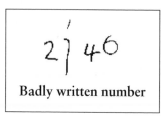

Badly written number

If an entry becomes illegible, such as through an ink blot or spilt coffee, the illegible entries should be copied with a cross-reference.

3. All amendments must leave the original figure legible

If you find that you have made a mistake in the accounting records, you must correct it so that the original figures are still legible. This usually means drawing a single line through the figures, and noting why the item has been deleted. As explained in the next section, it is preferable not to delete entries but to contra them.

How not to delete a cash book entry

How to delete a cash book entry

You never use opaque correction liquids on accounts. You never paste over the original paper. Never write over a figure to make it look like another figure. Always delete the original figure and enter the correct figure.

> Sundry Supplies   ˢ7 43
>
> **How not to correct a wrong figure**

4. An amendment usually requires <u>two</u> correcting entries

Suppose you enter £127 for an electricity bill, instead of £172. The best practice is to make one entry to reverse the incorrect entry, then make the correct entry. If you simply make *one* additional entry for the extra £45, your records will still agree and give the right answer. However, the records are not correct, as you did not receive electricity bills for £127 and £45; you received one bill for £172. It is not immediately obvious from the records to what the £45 refers.

If the two entries are close on the page, it is sufficient to mark the original entry and the reversal entry with the contra sign, ¢.

> Sundry Supplies   ¢ ˢ2 43
> ——— ᵘ ——— Correction ¢ (ˢ2 43)
> Sundry Supplies   ˢ7 43
>
> **How to correct an entry in a cash book**

Audit trail

A fundamental requirement of all accounting records is that they maintain what is known as the audit trail.

There are various **levels** of accounting records. Typically accounts have four levels:

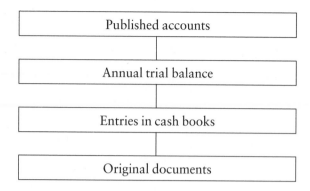

| Published accounts |
| Annual trial balance |
| Entries in cash books |
| Original documents |

This simply means that you can look at the records at any level in the accounts, and trace the figures up or down to any other level. For example, the published church accounts for 2006 say you spent £23,997 on building work. From this you look at the trial balance and see that it comprises these amounts:

February	£4,629.23
June	£11,204.16
November	£8,163.44
Total	£23,996.83

Note that whatever figure you find at one level must be there at the next level above or below in the accounts. Whatever figures are included in the published accounts must be present on the trial balance. No one should have to hunt or guess how any figure has been derived.

You turn to February's page in the cash book. There is a column headed 'Repairs and maintenance'. At the bottom of that column you see the total £4,629.23. In the column above, you see that there are three entries:

Date	Cheque	Folio	Details	Amount
11.2.12	003467	127	K. Bloggs	£2,429.14
19.2.12	003478	133	J. Spratt	£183.12
25.2.12	003502	149	F. Blenkinsop	£2,016.97
			Total	£4,629.23

You note that the figure of £4,629.23 found at trial balance level appears at the adjacent level. The column marked 'Folio' is your reference to the next layer down. You look in the file of bills for number 127, and find an invoice from K. Bloggs dated 9 January for:

Repairs to church window	
Fee as agreed	£2,067.35
plus 17.5% VAT	£361.79
Total	£2,429.14
Payable within 14 days.	

On the invoice the treasurer has written 127 in a circle in the top right-hand corner and 'Paid 11 February 2012' on the invoice.

You have now managed to go from the published accounts right back to one of the invoices.

Similarly, it is possible to follow the audit trail in the opposite direction. You could look at the invoice and see 'Paid 11 February 2006', which tells you where to find the item in the cash book. The cash book shows that this is included in the monthly total of £4,629.23. The trial balance shows that this total is included in the annual total of £23,996.83.

Vouchers

The lowest level of accounting record is the **voucher**. This is a document which gives the details of an item of income or expenditure. Normally the treasurer keeps two sets of vouchers:

- remittance advices (income)
- invoices (expenditure).

These documents are usually kept in lever-arch files in numerical order.

Sometimes it may be convenient to keep different types of voucher separately, such as keeping weekly cash sheets of collections in a separate folder from forms detailing other sources of income.

Every item of income and expenditure has a voucher unless its details are otherwise known. Two examples of the latter include:

- bank charges (which appear on the bank statement)
- transfers to or from other accounts (which match an equivalent entry in that account).

Sometimes the treasurer may need to create a voucher for the records. Vouchers may also comprise sheets prepared by other people, letters, statements, appeal literature or photocopies from other books. A voucher is any document which gives information about a payment.

Never pay a **statement** or reminder, nor regard either as an invoice. A statement is basically a list of unpaid invoices at a particular date. Statements are commonly issued about once a month by suppliers. Reminders are sent when an invoice is overdue. The purpose of a statement or reminder is to check that you have received all invoices. If you find that you are missing an invoice, ask for a copy.

One common reason for losing invoices is that they are sent with the goods and thrown away with the packaging. The best practice for suppliers is to send a **delivery note** with the goods, and send the invoice separately. However, not all suppliers do this. A delivery note simply allows the recipient to check that everything that should be there has been supplied. Once that check has been performed, the delivery note is no longer needed and can be discarded. Delivery notes are not part of the accounting system.

It is quite acceptable for invoices to be sent by fax or e-mail. It is not essential that an invoice must be a piece of paper sent by post.

Vouchers for the expenditure side usually take the form of **invoices**, sometimes called bills (though the word 'bill' can be applied to other documents). However, vouchers can take the form of receipts, letters, statements, tickets or other documents.

An invoice is not a demand to pay a sum: it is a statement that one party to a contract has completed his part and is entitled to payment. So an invoice is properly issued even when you have already paid for the work. Such invoices should have 'Invoice paid on 4 May 2012' or similar words on them, but this is not a legal requirement. If you receive an invoice for work already paid for but where this is not indicated, it may be advisable to check that your payment has been recorded.

Where a remittance advice does not comprise an invoice, it is necessary to show that the payment was properly incurred.

For a donation to a charity, a copy of a covering letter from the treasurer is probably the appropriate remittance advice. It clearly identifies the payment as a charitable donation and not a payment for a visiting speaker or supplies of literature.

For internal expenditure, such as reimbursing the minister's expenses or paying the choir, the voucher should be signed by the person you paid (particularly if paid in cash) or a note made when paying by cheque. Supporting paperwork should be attached as appropriate. For example, the minister should identify the categories of expenditure, such as stamps, coffee, petrol, etc. Some of these items may have vouchers, such as a receipt from the post office, supermarket or petrol station, stapled to the form or paper which notes the payment. These additional receipts should be filed when provided, but they are only normally required if the amount is particularly large or the expenditure unusual. A church may wish to set a limit when a receipt must be produced or may wish to state what items constitute usual or unusual expenditure. However, that is a matter for the church authorities.

For accounting purposes, there is no real difference between an invoice and an expenses claim. They can be kept in the same file or separately, as you prefer.

Occasionally, you may receive an expense claim with a huge pile of receipts attached. In such cases, it can be acceptable to note on the form that you have seen the receipts, and then throw them away.

Payment of the **choir** may comprise a photocopy of a page from the choir register on which the choirmaster has calculated the amount payable to each member. The treasurer should have sufficient details to know how much was payable to each member, even when the choirmaster makes the actual payment.

Sometimes a payment is accompanied by a **form**, such as payment of tax or insurance. In such cases, a photocopy of the form can serve as the document.

Sometimes one cheque may be written to pay for **several invoices**, such as when the church handyman has submitted four invoices for the four jobs he did that month. The four invoices should be stapled together under a single folio number. The principle of the audit trail applies even at this level, in that the figure entered in the cash book must appear on the document. The treasurer must produce a slip or piece of adding machine roll or write on the top invoice how the cash-book figure has been calculated.

Remittance advices

Church income usually comes from three main sources:

1 donations from church members by standing order or cheque
2 loose cash from collections
3 event income, such as magazine sales and hall lettings.

There is no need to create vouchers for every donation by stand-ing order or cheque: it is obvious from the cash book that these are donations. Loose cash will probably have a completed sheet identifying how much has been collected in each value of note and coin, with a date, time and signature. Other income may take the form of a covering letter from the magazine editor or a com-pleted form from the hall lettings secretary.

Record all income

Church income comes from various sources ranging from formal grants and tax refunds through to an envelope containing a few pounds from selling coffee after a special service. It must all be recorded.

The church treasurer must ensure that all income receivable is received, and all income received is recorded. It is not enough for the treasurer simply to record whatever is passed to him; the treasurer must be proactive in ensuring that church income is passed to him, or at least is accounted to him. The treasurer should be sufficiently knowledgeable of church life to know of flower festivals, concerts, outings and appeals, plus arrangements for refreshments, musicians, maintenance, hall bookings, chil-dren's and youth work, and any other aspect of church life which involves handling money. This will prevent difficult situations where someone in the church accumulates large funds of which the church authorities have no knowledge, or gets into a muddle and does not know how much has been received or spent.

A simple system should be introduced for all regular sources of income. For example, a hall booking secretary should provide the treasurer with a list of all regular bookings (such as scouts and health clubs), plus one-off bookings (such as birthday parties and wedding receptions). The treasurer can check that all such income has been received.

The magazine editor (or advertising manager) can provide a list of advertisers with agreed fees and when payable. The treasurer should check this against the actual advertisements in the magazine.

Refreshment and flower-arranging teams can fill in a simple form identifying how much they receive and spend each week.

Avoid situations where you have an envelope handed to you at inconvenient moments containing a few pounds from the sale of something after the service. If you know that someone is selling geraniums after the morning service to raise funds for the church, be proactive and give the person a simple form to record details for you.

Never mix church cash passed to you with your own cash. When given amounts of cash, always create a written record somewhere. Some treasurers keep a notebook for odd cash amounts, other treasurers carry a receipt book, and always issue a receipt. Neither is ideal, as there will inevitably be an occasion when you do not have your notebook or receipt book with you.

Collecting funds

A church typically has many sources of income. The treasurer must identify them all and ensure that money owed to the church is collected. Areas where this is likely to be an issue include:

- hall bookings
- rent from property
- interest, dividends and other income from investments
- magazine subscriptions
- magazine advertisements
- sales of refreshments after services
- income from bookstall and other sales
- fees for weddings and funerals.

A treasurer may have to be insistent that the respective officers do hand over the money. Sometimes people with responsibility in these areas may regard keeping the funds under their control as part of their duties. It must be made clear that legally they have no right to hold church funds against the wishes of the treasurer. In other words, other church officers should generally only hold church funds as a temporary measure until they can be passed to the treasurer.

In addition to regular sources of income, there will be one-off occasions such as concerts, festivals, fetes, fund-raising events and sale of church property (such as selling old hymn books or kneelers). This does not necessarily mean that the treasurer must act as debt collector for each of these items, but it does mean that the treasurer must ensure that someone is responsible for collecting money due, and does do so. If there is a problem collecting money due, the treasurer should report this to the appropriate church authorities who should consider what further steps to take.

The separate consideration of **bounced cheques** is considered on page 46.

Counting the collection

A church collection typically comprises donations in envelopes for regular giving plus loose cash. The treasurer will rarely be responsible for counting and banking the collection at every service. Usually this task is delegated to sidespeople, ushers or people specially deputed for the task.

Some basic disciplines for counting the collection are:

- the collection must be counted promptly after the end of each service
- two people must always be present when the collection is counted
- the loose cash is counted before the envelopes are opened
- the envelopes are opened, and the amounts recorded against the name or identifying number on the envelope, on a list
- a separate form is completed recording the total received in every different value of note and coin, whether from loose cash or envelopes
- notes are held together in bundles of £100 by rubber bands
- coins are bagged in cash bags provided free by banks in amounts of
   - £20 for £1 and £2 coins
   - £10 for 20p and 50p coins
   - £5 for 5p and 10p coins
   - £1 for 1p and 2p coins.

Do not mix coins of different values in the bag. Close the bag if it contains the full value, as indicated above. Leave the bag open if it contains less than the full value

- cheques, foreign coins and anything else which has monetary value are recorded separately on the form, and are only included in the total if they can be paid into a bank account
- keep the cash safe until it can be paid into the bank. It should either be kept in a safe, using a large cloth bag such as those which banks can be persuaded to provide free, or be taken home by the treasurer
- the form should be signed or initialled by both of those who counted the collection
- a record of the amount collected must be left at church premises.

Envelopes must have the amounts recorded in a manner which allows the donor to be identified, even if indirectly, such as against a list of numbers held by a stewardship secretary. This is not to check up on whether church members are 'paying their dues', but is an essential requirement for reclaiming income tax under Gift Aid; you may not know whether the donor had completed a Gift Aid form.

Paying money straight from the collection is not a good practice, and should be discouraged rather than banned. There is no problem if someone simply wants to change notes or coins from one value to another, such as handing over a £1 coin to have a stock of 10p coins as change when selling plants for 90p. You should discourage anyone from cashing a personal cheque from the collection.

If it is necessary to take money from the collection for any other purpose, such as to pay the choir or the refreshment team, ensure that full details are noted on the form. This will create a problem for your record keeping. If you received £200 and paid out £20, you will only bank £180 but must record £200 income and £20 payment. If a payment is made from the collection, it must be supported by such paperwork as is appropriate if you issued a cheque for the amount. See page 45. This means that those who count the collection will fill in two forms. First is the pledged giving form which can be as simple as the following:

Collection for service on   at

No. Amount	No. Amount	No. Amount	No. Amount

The second form is an analysis of the cash receipts. A typical form is shown in Figure 2.

Figure 2: Collection Analysis Form

Collection for service on   at

£20 notes	_____
£10 notes	_____
£5 notes	_____
£1 coins	_____
50p coins	_____
20p coins	_____
10p coins	_____
5p coins	_____
2p coins	_____
1p coins	_____
Other	_____
Sub-total	_____
Plus other income (please specify)	_____
Less payments (please specify	_____
TOTAL	_____

Signed _____ _____

The form above allows for all eventualities, including receiving cheques, £50 notes, Scottish and Irish banknotes and other items. It also allows for non-collection items to be added, though these should normally be separately accounted for. The form allows for payments to be made directly out of the collection, though this practice should also be discouraged. Notes on what constitutes legal tender are given on page 207.

Often someone other than the treasurer will arrange for the money to be paid in, usually on the Monday. It is then sufficient for that person to attach the paying-in counterfoil to the slip above and pass it to the treasurer.

Pledged giving

Churches increasingly rely on regular giving from members paid by standing order from the member's bank account to the church's. These matters are looked at in Chapter 17 on stewardship, usually administered by a separate stewardship secretary.

For the treasurer, the issues here are:

• that both the treasurer and pledged giving secretary want the bank statement for their records
• it is tedious for the treasurer to list each donation as a separate source of income
• identifying donors in the main church records can be seen as a breach of confidentiality or sensitivity.

A convenient approach is to have a separate bank account for receiving such donations by standing order. The balance can be transferred to the main bank account once a month as a single figure entered into the records. The separate bank account is still part of the church's accounts and so must be kept by the treasurer, but it makes it easier for both the treasurer and stewardship secretary to do their jobs.

Income in kind

Churches do not just receive cash, they also receive payments in kind through voluntary labour and gifts of assets.

Gifts of cash are always included in the church accounts.

Gifts of labour are not included in the accounts, although it is almost always the case that the church could not function without much voluntary work. If a church has a volunteer secretary, organist, youth worker, cleaner or whatever, the treasurer must resist any call to include a figure to reflect the value of that work. The church has not received that benefit in cash and it is false accounting to include it as such. Such a benefit would be difficult to value. Its inclusion would completely distort the accounts and destroy their purpose.

An exception to this may be needed if applying for a grant from certain bodies. In such cases, it may be appropriate to estimate the value of volunteer labour and treat this as both income in kind and expenditure in kind.

Gifts of assets for church use which are not consecrated or heritage assets usually are included in the accounts unless their value is small. Where someone gives a piano or computer to the church, that should be recognized as both income in kind and expenditure on the asset, which is usually a fixed asset. If an asset is donated for the church to sell, it is usually acceptable to include it only when sold, treating the sale proceeds as a receipt.

A church is not obliged to accept gifts they do not want. A church should not become a dump for old furniture and pianos.

Gifts may take the form of **intangible income** such as an interest-free loan, use of office space, temporary accommodation, professional services, and loan or free use of equipment. The general policy is that where the donor has borne expenses in providing the intangible income, an estimate of its value should be included as both income and expenditure. In other cases, the benefit should not be included. A discount or free business sample is not intangible income.

Trading income

In church accounting, **trading** means little more than incurring expenditure to receive income. It is not necessary that an activity has a commercial or fund-raising motive. Producing a magazine to promote the gospel is a trading activity if people are asked to pay for it or if it carries paid advertising. It is a trading activity even if priced so that it cannot make a surplus. Other trading activities may include concerts, fetes, hall lettings, refreshments, training and bookstalls. Each trading activity must be separately disclosed.

In the church accounts, the income and expenditure must be shown separately. It is not acceptable to net off these figures and show just a single figure of profit. An exception is if the income and expenditure is immaterial. If the youth club raises £4 for church funds by earning £5 from washing cars and spending £1 on materials, only the £4 needs to be added to income.

While this is clearly the correct accounting, it can lead to the objection that the accounts do not state how much profit or loss has been made by each trading activity. This is an area where accounts presentation must compromise between competing criteria. It is considered more important that church members can see the total income and total expenditure of the church. Seeing whether an activity is profitable involves no more than seeing if one number in the accounts is bigger than another.

MAKING PAYMENTS

Checking invoices and expenses

Before paying an invoice, the treasurer should check that:

- the items or service were properly ordered by the church
- the items or service were received by the church and are satisfactory
- the price agrees with what was quoted
- the arithmetic on the invoice is correct

The huge variety of invoices which can pass to a treasurer makes it almost impossible to produce prescriptive guidance which is sensible in all circumstances. The treasurer should decide how far he is satisfied that the first three conditions have been met. If necessary, the treasurer should ask another church officer to confirm the details and note this on the invoice. This may be a churchwarden confirming repairs to the boiler, or the Sunday school leader confirming an order for materials.

If goods were not ordered by the church at all, they are legally unsolicited goods, for which the law is explained on page 153.

In practice, a more likely problem is that a church member simply decided to order goods without appropriate authority. It is not unknown for clergy, church officers and non-officers simply to order goods without bothering to get authorization. In such circumstances, the treasurer should not pay the invoice but refer it to the church council (or equivalent body) to see if they will authorize the expenditure retrospectively. If they do, the invoice can be paid as normal. If the council decides not to pay the invoice retrospectively, the council could find itself in a legal dispute with the supplier, as explained on page 154. However, this is not an issue for the treasurer. The use of budgets, as explained on page 61, is a simple way to prevent such problems.

Checking that the goods were received and are satisfactory may mean checking with the officer who received the goods. In such a case, the details must be noted on the invoice. This may be a handwritten note saying '4.7.12 (John Smith) confirmed goods received OK'.

Checking the price quoted may mean checking against a purchase order or quotation for larger items. For many bills, this may be part of the same process as checking that the goods were received and are satisfactory.

Payments with order

Sometimes a cheque needs to be sent with a document where there is no invoice. Examples include insurance premiums and taxing vehicles. The treasurer should simply ensure that he has a photocopy of whatever document is completed and should use that as the invoice equivalent. The principle is that no cheque is issued without a document readily identifiable explaining what the payment is for.

Advances and IOUs

Sometimes a church may need to provide someone with funds before they have incurred expenditure. This may be to buy materials or as a float to pay for incidental expenses on a church outing.

An **advance** is perfectly acceptable in such situations, provided the ultimate expenditure is authorized and budgeted. The person to whom the money is advanced should be given a reasonable sum which may be slightly in excess of expected spending. The person should sign for the advance. That person should provide details of expenditure as soon as possible. Any excess funds should be returned to the treasurer. Any shortfall should be paid by the treasurer.

An advance is a remittance in its own right and should therefore have its own voucher. When the person has accounted for the expenditure, that accounting is another remittance or a receipt for which a separate voucher is prepared. This should be cross-referenced to the paperwork for the advance.

An **IOU** is when an individual borrows money. In general, IOUs should be discouraged. The church is not a money lender. Unless expressly authorized otherwise (which would be unusual), no one should borrow money on an IOU unless the minister or treasurer or some equivalent church officer has expressly authorized it.

If, say, a church employee finds that she has insufficient funds for her bus fare home, an IOU is probably tolerable, but this should not become a habit. In the High Court case *Sinclair v Neighbour [1967]*, the manager of a betting shop who earned £22 a week borrowed £15 from the till without permission. He put in an IOU and replaced the money the following day. When the employers discovered this, he was summarily dismissed (that is, without any notice and without any payment in lieu of notice). This was upheld by the court. This was a financial irregularity, and any financial irregularity from a person in a position of trust justifies summary dismissal.

A chuch should normally never lend money to an individual, but the church may consider a donation as explained on page 202. Many personal loans to help individuals are never repaid, which can cause difficulties to both parties. If made as a gift, the individual always has the option to repay.

Regular payments

All payments must be supported by paperwork sufficient to identify their nature and purpose. Some items, such as bank charges, appear on the bank statement without any supporting paperwork. Here the bank statement *is* the supporting paperwork. Other regular payments, such as leases or rent, may not have paperwork for each payment, but have a document in the treasurer's file to which the regular payments relate.

Analyse payments

The expenditure side of the accounts should be analysed into the categories you have already determined. You should be reluctant to create new categories.

The process of analysing expenditure can itself be problematic because most items of expenditure can be analysed in two ways:

1 by nature
2 by purpose.

For example, the wages of a youth worker could be analysed as either 'Wages and salaries' or 'Youth work'. Organ maintenance could be analysed as either 'Church maintenance' or 'Music'.

You should remember that the accounts are painting a picture. You must decide which is the more helpful analysis for church members. Are they more likely to be concerned at the total amount paid in all salaries or how much youth work costs? The answer is the latter. So, if you really cannot decide, choose a purposive analysis.

Cross-casting

The traditional method of analysing income and expenditure is using columns in a cash analysis book. Each (vertical) column represents an item of income or expenditure. The first three or four columns will give general information. This is:

- date (of payment or receipt)
- payee or payer, or nature of payment
- total amount of payment or receipt.

Sometimes a fourth column is added to relate it to the voucher number.

Each (horizontal) row analyses the total amount into the categories of income or expenditure. In many cases, the analysis will be to just one column.

Figure 3 is an example of what a page in a cash book may look like recording receipts.

Almost every amount listed on this page is analysed by a single figure in one column, but there are a few exceptions.

On 16.7.12, someone bought a book from the bookstall for £17.95. He paid by a £20 note and, when no one had change, he

Figure 3: Example of a page from a cash book recording receipts

Date	Item	Amount	Collec-tions	Pledged giving	Tax refund	Hall hire	Mag. sales	Refresh-ments	Book-stall	Invest-ments	Other
2.7.12	Collection	103.29	103.29								
2.7.12	Bookstall	12.38							12.38		
2.7.12	Refreshments	21.04						21.04			
5.7.12	Dog training	120.00				120.00					
9.7.12	Collection	98.40	98.40								
9.7.12	Bookstall	2.99							2.99		
9.7.12	Refreshments	18.32						18.32			
14.7.12	Brownies	280.60				280.60					
16.7.12	Collection	101.21	101.21								
16.7.12	Bookstall	20.00	2.05						17.95		
16.7.12	Refreshments	16.40						16.40			
17.7.12	Magazine sales	24.00					24.00				
18.7.12	J. Smith (party)	65.00				60.00			5.00		
23.7.12	Collection ¢	106.44	106.44								
23.7.12	Collection ¢	(106.44)	(106.44)								
23.7.12	Collection	104.66	104.66								
23.7.12	Refreshments	16.80						16.80			
23.7.12	Bookstall	3.99							3.99		
23.7.12	Refreshments	17.25						17.25			
24.7.12	D. Jones (wedding)	100.00				40.00					60.00
30.7.12	Collection	103.64	103.64								
30.7.12	Refreshments	6.31						16.31			(10.00)
31.7.12	Pledged giving	9871.20		9871.20							
Total		11,107.48	513.25	9871.20	—	500.60	24.00	106.12	42.31	—	50.00

said that the church could keep it. Arguably, you could say that the bookstall has made £20 worth of sales because the customer was prepared to overpay. It is probably more realistic to say that the extra £2.05 was a donation, which is how the item has been recorded.

On 18.7.12, John Smith came to the parish office to pay £60 to hire the hall for a birthday party. He noticed a book on the stall for £5, and gave one cheque to pay for them both. So his cheque for £65 is analysed as two figures.

On 23.7.12, you mistakenly entered the collection as £106.44 instead of £104.66. You don't alter the entry you have already made in ink. You reverse the entry below it, putting brackets round the figures to show that they are the other way round; they are negative numbers. The original wrong entry and the matching correction are indicated by the contra symbol ¢ to make clear what has happened. Contra entries should still be analysed. The correct entry is then entered without any crossing out, scribbles or opaque correction fluid.

On 24.7.12, David Jones paid £100 in respect of his wedding fees. Of this £40 was the balance to hire the hall for a reception, and £60 was to pay the organist. This latter payment goes into 'Other' as we do not have a column for organist fees. If we had an 'Agency' column (see page 8), this payment could go there, as the whole £60 is paid out again.

On 30.7.12, the refreshments team took £16.31 but the supervisor took out £10 to buy some more coffee. This is not good practice. The supervisor should pay in the whole £16.31 and the treasurer provide funds for her to buy more coffee. However, that is the ideal world rather than the real world. The treasurer banks the balance of £6.31 and analyses that the takings were £16.31 and then shows £10 with brackets round. This means that the figure is the other way round from normal. Instead of this being money coming in, it is money going out. It is a negative figure. That is why the total for 'Other' is £50. You have added £60 to minus £10.

Each column of figures is added to give a **sub-total**. A sub-total is a sum of numbers which is itself to be added to other numbers. It is advisable to write all these sub-totals in pencil. The sub-totals for the columns from 'Collections' to 'Other' when added together should equal the total under 'Amount' as both figures represent the total of all the numbers you have entered in the cash analysis. The problem is that often they do not. This means that you have a mistake which must be found.

Sometimes the entries will not fit on a single page of a cash book. When this happens, the sub-totals, known as **running totals**, are produced for the first page. When balanced, as explained below, these sub-totals are marked '**Carried forward**', commonly abbreviated to 'c/fwd'. Exactly the same numbers are entered at the top of the next page with the narrative '**Brought forward**', commonly abbreviated to 'b/fwd'. This process can be repeated indefinitely over as many pages as needed.

It is advisable to add up figures using an adding machine which produces a till roll. This way you can check that your entries are correct. When using an adding machine, you may find a selector switch which says something like 'A0234F'. The setting should be on 'A' for adding machine. (The numbers indicate the number of decimal places in arithmetical calculations, where F means full display for as many decimal places as the machine can display.) There may be another selector switch with positions P and NP for print and non-print. You should set it to P. You must remember that whole amounts of pounds are entered using the 'oo' button, so £12.00 is entered as 12. At the end of each addition, you press the key marked * which produces the total, even though this may already be displayed. If you do not press this key, the old total may be added into the next total. A further complication is that on adding machines and calculators the keys are in a different order from a telephone, with 1, 2, 3 at the bottom rather than the top. All these disciplines soon become second nature.

Before adding machines were invented, book-keepers developed considerable mental arithmetic skills, and could calculate sub-totals in their head in a few seconds. Even though such skills are not needed now, it is still good practice to check that the sub-total is credible. It is easy to enter the hall hire figure of £280.60 as £28060.00, which would give a ludicrous sub-total £28,280.00 for hall hire for the month.

If you have produced a till roll, it is a simple matter to check that all figures have been entered correctly. It may console you to know that when the author first typed the sample page above, the sub-total for 'Amount' was 11,048.98 because the figure of 65.00 had been entered as 6.50.

If the mistake cannot easily be found, there is an old book-keeping skill called **difference-finding.** You find the difference between the total under 'Amount' and the figure from adding the other sub-totals together. If the difference is a multiple of 9, this can indicate that two numbers have been reversed in the cash analysis, such as analysing £753 as £573. If you divide the difference by 9, you find the difference between the two figures which have been reversed, and the number of zeros after this figure tells you where that difference occurs. In our example, the difference is £180, of which one-ninth is £20. This indicates that there is a difference of 2 between the hundreds and tens digits. Your eyes can scan the page for figures where there is a difference of two between consecutive digits in that position to see if they have been correctly analysed.

If the difference is a multiple of 10, this can indicate that a digit has been incorrectly written in the analysis. For example, suppose you analysed £358 as £368. You check down the page to see if all the figures have been correctly analysed.

If the difference is a specific figure, say £27.81, this can indicate that you forgot to analyse that figure. You scan the page to see if that figure appears.

These short cuts, which are simpler to understand than to explain, are effective in dealing with a single obvious mistake. If there is more than one mistake, these methods may not help. Sometimes a page of a cash book refuses to balance. You can become 'number blind' in hunting for the difference as the eyes start to see what they want to see. The procedure for a page which will obstinately not agree is:

- check all cross-casting to see that each row has been fully analysed
- add up all columns again, covering up your previous sub-total
- put a piece of paper about halfway down the page and add up half the column, and then the other half. This narrows down where the difference occurs
- if all else fails, leave it, and return the following day when in five seconds you may find the discrepancy that eluded you for 30 minutes.

These disciplines may appear not to be necessary in the modern world of computer accounts programs. However, these disciplines can still be needed. Difference-hunting can be needed when performing a bank reconciliation in Microsoft Money, for example.

Petty cash

It is reasonable and quite acceptable for a church to have a petty cash account, provided it is properly controlled. These controls are:

- the petty cash is kept on church premises in a secure place
- it does not hold unnecessarily large amounts of cash
- cash is kept with sufficient quantities of notes and coins of different denominations
- there is a list of those authorized to draw from petty cash
- every withdrawal is supported by a completed and signed petty cash voucher left in the box. Such vouchers can be bought inexpensively from local stationers.

Petty cash is operated on either the float basis or imprest system. Under the **float system,** a cheque is periodically cashed at the bank in whatever notes and coins are appropriate and added to the box. Under the **imprest system** the box is topped up by the value of vouchers since the last top-up. Thus the value of cash plus vouchers always equals the same figure. This does not really represent any improvement in security over the simpler float system.

Petty cash should not be used for payments which could easily be made by cheque or standing order. Petty cash is for paying the milk bill and buying glue and coffee.

There is no great objection to someone simply exchanging currency of one denomination for another, such as changing a £5 note into five £1 coins. Otherwise petty cash should not be used for cashing cheques or lending money.

The treasurer should periodically remove the vouchers and write them in the petty cash book or computer equivalent. The petty cash should also be counted periodically, at least once a month, to see that the balance agrees. It rarely does. This does not necessarily mean that anything is necessarily untoward; provided discrepancies are small and vary between being overstated and understated, there is no cause for concern. The difference is entered into the petty cash book, usually as a 'sundry' expenditure or income, so that the petty cash again agrees.

Even a large discrepancy of say £50 does not necessarily mean that anything improper is happening. The minister could have been reimbursing himself for an expense when suddenly called away before completing the voucher. Reasonable enquiries will usually determine if this is the case, allowing the records to be corrected.

If the treasurer does have concern about how petty cash is being used, that concern should be raised with the church council or equivalent. The treasurer should not make any decisions on its operation.

Computer software

For all but the simplest financial arrangements, a computer should be used. Computers themselves (the hardware) can now be bought for less than £1,000, while accounting software can be bought for £100 or less.

The government has promoted the use of computers and since 6 April 2009 it has been illegal to pay over income tax and national insurance from a payroll other than electronically. This means that payroll must be run on a computer, which is now almost essential anyway.

A computer is simply a tool, like a fountain pen. It does not think or make decisions, but obediently follows your instructions and those written into its programs. A computer error is better described as a computer operator error. There is a computing term known as GIGO – garbage in, garbage out. It means that the quality of computer output depends on computer input.

A computer simply automates the procedures that were previously done manually. It even uses the same terms, such as 'folders' and 'documents', for its electronic equivalents.

If you have no experience of computers, it is worth learning, as so much of everyday life is now computer based. The best way to learn is to:

- buy a computer but get someone else to set it up
- have someone show you how to use it (don't try to follow the often incomprehensible instructions)
- start with something simple, such as producing a document, and then learn one new trick at a time
- practise using the computer, and try to work out answers to problems before asking for help
- ask for help if you cannot resolve an issue for yourself.

Don't be embarrassed to acknowledge that your grandchildren may have a better grasp than you, and may be happy to explain it to you.

There is no objection to a treasurer keeping church records on his own computer, provided the records are kept entirely separate from the treasurer's personal records. If you need to acquire a computer or accounting software, there is probably a computer specialist in your congregation who can advise. If not, there may be accountants and others who keep financial records who can help.

When acquiring any software, you should consider more than just what it does and how much it costs. You must also consider what support you will get in the future, and whether the software will be kept up to date. Software is updated in two ways: compliance updating, and specification updating. The first, **compliance updating**, is to reflect changes in law and accounting standards. The second, **specification updating**, is simply to add more functions – colloquially known as 'bells and whistles'. You need the former, but probably not the latter. A computer or software should not be regarded as obsolete just because there is a later version. If they still do what you want and comply with current regulations, there is no reason to discard them. For specification updating, it is usually sufficient to review what products are available every five years or so.

Software often comes with many functions that may not always be needed. For this reason it is common for software to be supplied with a 'wizard' which allows you to choose which functions you want. Wizards usually have a standard setting which is appropriate for most purposes and should be selected when starting. You can always adjust the scope of the wizard later.

Remember that, when you buy software, you are buying a licence to use that software and must comply with the terms of the licence. This usually means that you may only load and use that software on one computer, other than as a back-up. You must not allow or use unauthorized copies, commonly known as 'grey software'. This is a form of theft. If you do need several copies of software, the supplier will usually sell you a group licence.

Accounting software

In terms of software, you should be clear at the outset what you want the computer to do. We are assuming that you already have basic software such as Word for producing written text, and Excel for producing spreadsheets.

If you simply want the computer to keep track of bank accounts and cash, Microsoft Money is adequate. This may be provided as part of the Microsoft Windows package when you first acquired the computer. Money allows you to produce reports from which annual accounts can usually be easily prepared, but they do not allow you to prepare the final accounts themselves.

There are plenty of other accounting software packages available, but it is unlikely that they will contain many additional features required by a church treasurer.

One program specifically designed for churches and charities is **Finance Co-Ordinator,** produced by Data Developments, Wolverhampton Science Park, Stafford Road, Wolverhampton, West Midlands WV10 9RU. Telephone: 01902-824044, e-mail: sales@data-developments.co.uk, website: www.data-developments. co.uk. This is designed to ensure compliance with charity law and accounting standards, and is specifically designed for fund-based non-commercial organizations. The company has been providing this software since 1985, and so is likely to remain in business, which has not always been the case with such software. It allows for restricted and unrestricted funds, endowments, statement of financial activity (SOFA) reports, and the suchlike. The software also produces management reports.

Payroll

A payroll for a church is not significantly different from a payroll for a commercial business. So there is no need for special payroll software for churches or charities.

There are many inexpensive but versatile payroll software packages on the market from reliable and established suppliers. Many offer additional functions such as personnel records, time and attendance, and human resources management, which are unlikely to be needed by church treasurers.

3

Banking

Introduction

Strictly speaking, a church does not need a bank account at all but could keep all its funds in ready cash. This is not recommended because of the security risk and lack of reliable documentation. However, it can be useful for a church to keep a small amount of 'petty cash' available, as explained on page 37.

A church will normally have at least two bank accounts:

- a current account for day-to-day expenditure
- a deposit account where funds not immediately needed can earn interest.

There are other reasons why it may be convenient to have more than one bank account:

- a separate account to receive pledged gifts can considerably simplify the procedure and also help protect the confidentiality of the donors (see page 27)
- a separate account should be used when making charitable payments, particularly to overseas countries, to prevent fraud (see page 193)
- a second bank account is always useful should you get into problems with your first bank and be unable to use that account while the problem is being solved.

It is not necessary to have a bank account for every fund. Funds can be distinguished in the records. For example, a deposit account containing £10,000 may represent a building maintenance fund of £4,000, a roof repair fund of £5,000 and an organ fund of £1,000.

Bank services

The functions you need from a bank are to:

- look after your funds
- provide cash when needed (such as floats for a fete)
- provide a cheque book
- provide monthly statements.

Banks can offer other services, such as:

- safe custody of documents
- placing spare funds on money market
- buying shares and some other investments
- lending money.

Increasingly banks are offering Internet services, where you can look at your account at any time of the day or night using a computer. There are some banks which use only the Internet.

Choosing a bank

The only bank which seems to be interested in providing banking services for churches is the **Reliance Bank**, owned by the Salvation Army.

A bank account, like an insurance policy, is a financial product. Your attitude to choosing a bank should be the same as choosing the supplier of any other product. Some guidance on this is given on page 155. It is a curiosity that a church may go to great lengths to check out the terms and credibility of a supplier of a photocopier or window, but give little or no consideration on which bank to use.

For this book, the author did his own form of a *Which?* report by writing to the press offices of twenty-one banks asking them a few questions and requesting literature. The banks were:

Abbey National (now Santander)	Bank of Scotland
	Barclays Bank
Alliance & Leicester (now Santander)	Clydesdale Bank
	Co-operative Bank
Allied Irish Bank	First Direct
Bank of Ireland	Girobank

Halifax (HBOS)	Royal Bank of Scotland
HFC Bank	Standard Chartered
HSBC	Virgin One
Lloyds TSB	Woolwich (now part of
NatWest	Barclays)
Reliance Bank	Yorkshire Bank

Alone among these twenty-one banks, Reliance replied within one week and answered all my questions. The other twenty banks had not replied within one month, apart from Barclays, whose commercial department returned my letter with a covering note saying they could not answer my question because I had not quoted my account number! They had obviously not even bothered to read the letter. When the twenty banks were chased up by telephone calls, a few apathetic responses were eventually generated, though not one bank could be bothered to post a single piece of literature. Even the Co-operative Bank was not. After a process akin to pulling teeth with tweezers, four banks provided a few details, though none provided all the details requested.

This point about UK banks is emphasized because a business which does not look after you before you are a customer will certainly not look after you when you are. If a bank is unhelpful to an author, you can be sure it will be unhelpful to his readers.

Reliance Bank advises that it welcomes accounts from churches, and already has 900 as customers. It develops a tariff for each customer based on current banking activity. For a new church, it will consider six months' free banking. It follows the ethical policies of the Salvation Army. The bank offers cheque book and paying-in books, facilities for standing orders and direct debits, regular statements, Internet banking, savings accounts, telegraphic transfers by BACS and CHAPS, and foreign currency services.

Mandate

The mandate is your instructions to the bank of who may sign cheques and give other instructions to the bank. This is a decision to be made by the local church authorities, subject to any restrictions imposed by the bank. Keep the mandate simple. Suggested arrangements are to have no more than three signatories

– perhaps the treasurer, the minister and a senior officer who lives near the treasurer or is readily accessible to the treasurer; and to have a limit of perhaps £250 below which only one signature is needed, and above which two out of three signatures are needed.

Churches and other organizations can often get into great difficulties over bank mandates, particularly when officers change.

There is no objection to the treasurer being a signatory. Sometimes churches want two signatures on every cheque, which is also acceptable practice.

A treasurer should never regard any requirement for a second signature as reflecting on the treasurer's reputation. If the church had the faintest doubt about your competence or integrity, you would not be the treasurer in the first place. All the controls are designed not to check up on you, but to:

- demonstrate to the church the high standards maintained by the church in its financial arrangements
- reassure the auditor or examiner (and possibly reduce the audit bill)
- provide disciplines which help to prevent error.

The signature should be the person's normal signature. Legible signatures are harder to forge than illegible squiggles and therefore provide greater security.

The mandate must be supported by a formal resolution of the church council or equivalent body formally appointing those people as signatories. The bank may require a copy of the resolution signed by the church council secretary or minister.

The signatories must then prove their identity to the bank. This is not the banks being awkward, but is a legal requirement under money laundering regulations. Signatories must attend the bank in person by appointment, taking identity such as passports or driving licences.

A church must always be alert to any change of signatories. There have been instances where churches have had problems accessing their funds because signatories have changed. A church must always be prompt in removing old signatories, and completing a new mandate to add new signatories.

Issuing cheques

A cheque must only be issued if the treasurer is satisfied that it has been properly authorized. In practice this means that the payment arises:

- from a specific resolution of the church council
- from a legal agreement made by the church council
- within a budget allocated to a particular church officer (such as allowing the youth leader to spend £1,000 a year).

A cheque is normally completed using a cheque book provided for the purpose. This normally contains the name of the church, the account number, the sorting code, the bank's name and address, and a cheque number. The bottom of the cheque gives, in order:

- the number of the cheque (six digits)
- the sorting code (six digits, expressed as three pairs)
- the account number (eight digits).

These are printed in magnetic ink using a stylized typeface such as OCRA (optical character reading 'A') to allow cheques to be automatically read. These numbers sometimes appear with other marks. When the cheque is presented for payment, the amount is typed on in the same typeface, allowing the appropriate accounts to be cleared automatically.

The cheque must be completed by the payer, who adds:

- the name of the payee (who you are paying)
- the amount of the payment, in words and figures
- the date of the cheque
- signature.

The cheque must be completed in ink, which includes rubber stamps (not recommended, but legal) and printing from computers or other machines. Cheque books and any rubber stamps must be keep secure when not in use.

In writing out the amount in words, odd pence may be indicated numerically, such as 'One hundred and forty-nine pounds 26' for £149.26. It is advisable for lines to be drawn to fill in the spaces after the payee and amount to prevent additional figures being added.

The date is usually written in numerical form of day, month, year. Note that the USA uses the convention of month, day, year, so 1 March 2012 is 01.03.12 in the UK, but 03.01.12 in the USA.

Strictly speaking, a cheque does not need to be issued using a cheque book provided by the bank. It is legal to issue a cheque on a piece of plain paper, or using someone else's cheque book, or even writing a cheque on an inanimate object. Cheques have been presented written on paving stones and dustbin lids, usually as a form of protest or publicity stunt. However, such practices are not recommended. There can be an increased risk of error, and there will certainly be additional bank charges.

One point cannot be made too strongly: **a signatory must never sign a blank cheque.** There are no exceptions to this absolute rule. Signing a few blank cheques may seem the sensible thing to do when the treasurer is going on holiday, but it is a form of fraud on the church in that the signatory is flouting the required security for issue of cheques. An auditor who discovers such a practice should report this. The church should have sufficient signatories to cover temporary absences. If necessary, an additional signatory can be created for a specific period.

Bank charges

The treasurer must always know the basis of bank charges, including the charge for paying in cash, as churches may handle considerable quantities of coins. Bank charges of £25 a month may not seem much until you realise that is £300 a year.

Bank charges become very steep for any bank if you incur an **unauthorised overdraft**. Interest is also charged at a high rate, often above 25%.

The bank is not obliged to pay cheques which exceed the balance in your account or an agreed overdraft. If you do exceed the limit, the bank may dishonour or 'bounce' your cheque. This is not only embarrassing to the church, but also incurs a charge. The charge can exceed the cheque that is dishonoured. You also pay interest at a much higher rate. Banks are usually coy about disclosing overdraft rates in sales literature, and usually only provide details in branches.

Although most banks now use the Faster Payments process and funds are usually transferred in a few hours, the treasurer must remember that cheques may take three days to clear. Also, charges can easily put a bank account into overdraft before you are aware of the problem. Suppose you issue a £10 cheque believing that you have £40 in the account, but unknown to you the bank has just deducted £31 in bank charges. As you have only £9 in the account, the bank returns the cheque and deducts another £30. Because this puts your account in overdraft, it charges £12.50. You have been hit for £42.50 charges plus high interest of perhaps £2.50 for the few days giving a total of £45 – and you still have to pay £10 and explain why your cheque bounced.

In addition to bank charges, it is easy for a treasurer to overlook a payment when keeping a record of the balance on the account. It is also possible that a cheque which you pay in may not be honoured and so your account does not receive the funds you expect.

The moral is not to run the bank account too low – for example by transferring too much to a deposit account. Have a **buffer** of perhaps £250 below which you do not allow the account to fall. This provides a safety margin, and prevents unpleasant surprises. It is true that you will lose interest, but the amount is small.

There are other perhaps more acceptable methods for reducing bank charges:

- use electronic banking (explained below) where the charges are often much lower, and where you can keep a closer eye on your account without having to wait for the statement to arrive
- use a payment card or charge card, where the charges are usually lower than writing a cheque
- keep petty cash and use that for paying small bills, such as the milkman
- pay regular payments by direct debit
- draw cash from a machine operated by your bank rather than cashing a cheque over the counter (though you will not be able to obtain notes and coins in the denomination you want)
- pay cheques in batches rather than individually
- pay as infrequently as possible, such as quarterly rather than monthly, or monthly rather than weekly
- pay some of the collection into petty cash rather than into the bank
- ask donors to pay you by standing order.

Internet banking

Anyone with a computer connected to the Internet can enjoy the benefits of Internet banking, namely:

- lower bank charges
- ready access to statements at any time of the day
- an ability to leave messages and transact some business.

There are some bank accounts such as Egg which only operate on the Internet. Most ordinary cheque book accounts come with an Internet access facility, making it an Internet account. You are given a website address to log into. Typically, you are given a user identification number of eight or more digits and letters. You choose a password which should not be anything memorable or obvious, and should be changed periodically. Typically the program asks you to select key letters from your password from a list offered to you. Suppose you chose Ezekiel as your password. The computer may ask you for the second, fourth and fifth letters. So you scroll down three lists of the alphabet to select Z, K and I. If you get it wrong, it will usually allow you one more go before barring further attempts. Otherwise someone who obtained your identification number from seeing the card on your desk could try all the books in the Bible and other likely words until getting lucky.

Internet services on a bank account are usually provided free by the bank, as it considerably reduces their costs.

Payment cards

Banks usually now provide free payment cards or debit cards to customers, including business customers and churches. These are the same size as credit cards but work differently.

The payment is debited from your account when you make the payment. There is no bill to pay as with credit cards. It is vital that a strict control is kept over such cards and that the church authorities approve the treasurer having one. In effect, the treasurer is given unlimited signing power on the account.

In 2005, banks introduced **chip and pin** cards. Instead of signing a slip of paper, the customer enters four digits into a machine. If the PIN number is correct, the payment is authorized. For this reason, the PIN number should not be obvious, such as your date of birth. It can also be changed periodically in the bank's cash machines. Perhaps the best mnemonic for a PIN number is to remember a four-word phrase where the number of letters in each word is the number. So 'the forgiveness of sins' indicates 3024 (counting a ten-lettered word as 0).

Bank statements

The bank issues a statement, usually monthly, listing all payments into and out of the account and showing a balance. Banks usually provide folders in which to keep statements. The statements should be immediately filed in the folder, with the latest statement on top.

The bank statement is needed to:

- identify receipts and payments not already recorded
- check that payments and receipts are in order, and question any which appear not to be
- perform a bank reconciliation, explained below.

Bank statements often include items which you have not already recorded in your cash books. These items can be either payments or receipts. A church bank account will probably have many standing orders from donors. There may be regular payments from a bank account by standing order or direct debit, such as regular lease payments. Other items can include interest on the account and bank charges. All these items are usually picked up when performing the first part of the bank reconciliation.

Bank reconciliation

In your cash books, you record the amount of cash the church has in its bank account. This is after all the cheques have been issued and all the payments in have been cleared.

In terms of day-to-day funds, this is a theoretical figure as there is always a time lag between issuing a cheque and when the amount is taken from the account. The cheque may have to arrive by post, the person may not pay it in immediately, and then it takes a few days to clear. Many treasurers can be surprised at how long it takes some people to pay in cheques they issue. Some cheques never get paid in. Conversely, there can be a delay, usually much shorter, before payments into the bank are added to the account. The consequence of all this is that the balance shown on the bank statement is different, and usually higher, than the equivalent figure from your cash books.

To provide a check on the accounts, it is usual to perform a bank reconciliation for each statement you receive. This reconciles the closing balance on the bank statement with the figure you have from your cash books.

This principle is best understood by a simple example. Suppose you open an account on 1 January 2012 and make the following payments and receipts.

		Dr	Cr
3.1.12	Payment into account	200.00	
6.1.12	Cheque 000001		23.46
8.1.12	Cheque 000002		15.63
25.1.12	Cheque 000003		100.42
26.1.12	Payment into account	40.00	
28.1.12	Cheque 000004		12.46
Payments in		240.00	
Less cheques			151.97
Balance as at 31.1.12		88.03	

This simple account shows us that we paid £240 into the bank, and issued four cheques which total £151.97, so we have £88.03 in the bank. However, the bank statement looks rather different:

Account Activity

Date	Payment type	Details	Paid out £	Paid in £	Balance £
5.1.12	Giro Credit	500001		200.00	200.00
12.1.12	Cheque	000002	15.63		184.37
28.1.12	Cheque	000003	100.42		83.95

According to the cash book, you have £88.03 in the bank at the end of the month, but the bank says that you only have £83.95. The explanation is obvious: one payment and two cheques had not cleared. The bank reconciliation simply lists these items to check that the figures agree.

Some points to remember in a bank reconciliation:

- you reconcile the bank statement to your cash book, not the other way round. It is your cash book that has the 'correct' figure for your purposes
- you check off items in the cash book against their appearance on the bank statement, usually by putting a little tick against the figures on each
- items on the bank statement which do not appear in your cash book are added to your cash book as receipts or payments. You then check off the items with little ticks. These can include standing orders paid in or out, bank charges paid out, and interest paid in
- at this stage every item on the bank statement should have a little tick against it. You then *subtract* uncleared cheques and other payments, and *add* uncleared receipts.

In our example above, the bank reconciliation will look like this:

St Gertrude's Bank Reconciliation for January 2012

Balance per bank statement		£83.95
plus receipts not cleared		£40.00
		£123.95
less cheques not cleared:		
000001	£23.46	
000004	£12.46	
		£35.92
Balance per cash book		£88.03

Note that the correct figure for our purposes is the cash book figure of £88.03. The bank reconciliation simply shows how the different figure on the bank statement is the equivalent of that cash book figure.

The process of performing a bank reconciliation is an essential discipline in checking that your cash book is correct, that all payments and receipts in your account have been recorded, that the bank statement is correct, and what cheques have yet to be cleared.

There are a few further points to note about bank reconciliations. The method above is fine for the first month of an account or when all cheques are cleared promptly. In other cases, going back months in a cash book can be tedious and lead to errors. It is therefore usual to tick only the cash book for *the current month*, and the previous bank reconciliation for all previous months. The bank reconciliation for the previous month lists all uncleared items, most of which have probably cleared in the current month. The items you add or subtract in the current month's bank reconciliation are therefore the unticked items from the current month's cash book and last month's bank reconciliation.

Stale cheques

If a cheque is more than six months old, it has become a **stale cheque**. This means that the time for paying it in has expired. If the payee does try to pay it in, the bank will reject it (or at least, the bank *should* do). A stale cheque is shown as an uncleared cheque in the month it becomes six months old. In the following month, the cheque is written back in your cash book. It is shown in the payments section but as a negative payment, such as by putting brackets round the numbers, and is subtracted from the total. This entry and the original must be cross-referenced by contra sign to each other.

The fact that a cheque has gone stale does not mean that you no longer owe the money and can regard this non-payment as bunce. The treasurer should try to contact the payee and usually arrange for a replacement cheque to be issued. The payee may have lost the cheque, forgotten about it, or had it stolen. Don't issue a replacement cheque until contact has been made with the payee. It is possible that the payee has moved, died, emigrated or simply disappeared.

Sometimes an item appears on a bank statement as both 'paid in' and 'paid out'. This happens if you pay in a cheque which bounces but clears on re-presentation. Another example is where the bank imposes a charge which it then agrees to refund. If the same amount appears in each column of the bank statement for the same item, you tick each of them on the bank statement. The two entries are contras, as explained on page 17.

Sometimes you may find that an item appears on the bank statement which should not. This is a rare occurrence, but it has been known for the banking system to clear items to or from the wrong account. It is also known for a crook to try to get money from your account. If you find any entry on the bank statement which you do not understand, you must contact the bank immediately. If there is evidence that the account is being fraudulently raided, the bank will have specific procedures to deal with the matter. If you have not authorized the payments, the bank is liable to refund the wrongful payments.

Sometimes you may find that an item appears on the bank statement for a different amount. For example, you may have recorded a cheque for £25.00 when the bank shows it as £35.00. Such cases are rare. If it does happen, you should first check that your cash book is correct and that you have not simply entered the wrong figure. If you are correct, for the bank reconciliation, the difference is added to or subtracted from the bank total. The matter should be raised with the bank.

Stolen or lost cheques

If a cheque book goes missing, you must report it to the bank immediately. Always assume that a missing cheque book is stolen until you find out otherwise. The bank will stop payments on the account until the matter is resolved. This can cause problems because an innocent payee can find that your cheque to him is dishonoured in the meantime. You should explain to the payee what has happened. If necessary, take the cheque back and possibly make payment in another way, such as by cash or from another bank account.

Stopped cheques

A cheque can be stopped by you at any time until payment has been made by your bank. Therefore, if you need to stop a cheque, you should do so promptly.

For reasons explained below, stopping a cheque should only be done for a good reason. You stop a cheque by telephoning the bank and confirming your instructions in writing. You should normally contact the payee immediately after telling the bank and ask them to return the cheque to you. The bank will want to know why you wish to stop a cheque. The legal term for stopping a cheque is a 'countermand'. The law is contained in Bills of Exchange Act 1882 s.75. The bank is under a duty to check that the countermand came from the customer, and not to countermand if there is any doubt.

Legal status of cheques

A cheque is legally defined as "a bill of exchange drawn on a banker payable on demand" (Bills of Exchange Act 1882 s73). It is an instruction to your bank to pay an amount to a person (usually to their bank account) from your funds with the bank.

Cheques were first used in 1680, but became much more sophisticated during the 20th century with special forms, account names and numbers added, and optical character reading provided. Strictly speaking, there is no need to use a cheque book at all to issue a cheque. A cheque may legally be written on plain paper or indeed on any other surface. This is not recommended practice as it delays payment and can incur significant charges.

A cheque may be **crossed**. This may be a **general crossing** or a **special crossing**. A cheque which is not crossed is said to be an **open cheque.**

An open cheque is now very rare. It does not contain two parallel lines across the payee and amount. In effect it is a bearer bill with little more security than a bank note. Someone with an open cheque can walk into the bank and receive payment for the amount stated.

A crossed cheque has two parallel lines either vertical or diagonally against the writing of the payee and amount. The lines may be printed or written. This means that the cheque can only be paid into a bank account, and not cashed unless the cheque is made out to "cash". A crossed cheque must be paid into an account in the name of the payee unless **negotiated,** which means that the payee has written on the back "pay [another name]" and signed it. The cheque then becomes payable to the other name.

A cheque may be specially crossed, by writing between the parallel lines either the name of a bank or a place (or both), meaning that the cheque can only be paid into an account at that bank or in that place.

In practice, today most cheques are crossed with the words **"account payee"** written in the crossing. From 16 June 1992 this has legal effect in meaning that the cheque can only be paid into an account with the payee's name; the cheque cannot be negotiated.

Standing orders and direct debits

Standing orders and direct debits are means by which regular payments are automatically made by the bank to or from your account. Either method may be set up in writing, by telephone or using the Internet.

A church will usually receive regular payments by standing order from church members. It is most unlikely that a church will be allowed to receive funds by direct debit.

A church may make payments by standing order, such as if supporting a missionary, renting property or leasing equipment. It may make payments by direct debit for telephone and electricity bills.

A **standing order** is a regular payment *of the same amount* paid at regular intervals, such as on the 4th of each month, or every Friday, or on the first Monday of each quarter. A standing order may be paid into any account. If the amount of a standing order is to be changed, a new standing order must be arranged by the payer.

A **direct debit** is a regular payment *of a variable amount*. This is ideal for services where the charge varies from period to period, such as for utility bills. Because you are allowing someone else to determine how much money they take from your account, direct debits are more strictly controlled than standing orders. The main points are:

- the payer must be notified of the amount at least ten working days before the payment is taken
- direct debit may only be used by businesses and other bodies which comply with a strict evaluation for 'integrity, sound financial standing and administrative capability'
- a full and immediate refund must be made if an amount is taken in error.

Direct debits are overseen by BACS (Bankers Automated Credit Service) owned by the main clearing banks.

A bank customer has the right to cancel a standing order or direct debit at any time. In practice, it can sometimes be difficult cancelling a direct debit, and you could find yourself having to be insistent with the bank.

Direct debits are convenient for suppliers as it simplifies their accounting process, and avoids the needs to issue reminders and chase up debts.

Another practical advantage is that direct debit avoids the risk of a bill being overlooked or lost in the post, with the consequent risk of loss of services or additional charges. Over half of the adult population of the UK uses direct debit.

You must ensure sufficient funds are in the account when the standing order or direct debit is presented for payment. If there are insufficient funds, the standing order or direct debit is dishonoured (or 'bounced'). Some organizations will re-present the order or debit to see if funds have appeared, but many organizations do not re-present. Some automatically cancel a direct debit if it is dishonoured.

Standing orders and direct debits are paid on banking days. When a regular day, such as 1st of the month, is not a banking day, the payment is made on the next banking day. Banking days are all Mondays to Fridays, other than bank holidays.

Cancelling a direct debit or a standing order does not in itself mean that you have cancelled the service to which it relates. If you wish a telephone line to be disconnected, for example, you must notify the telephone company, giving the required notice period. Until that notice period has expired, you remain liable to pay the bill by some other means, probably by cheque. If a reduction in the bill has been given for payment by direct debit, that will be lost.

A direct debit is automatically cancelled if no payment is made under it for thirteen months, known as the 'dormancy period'.

Overdrafts

An overdraft is when the bank allows a customer to make payments from an account when there is insufficient money in the account to cover the payment.

If there is sufficient money in the account to honour a cheque or other payment instruction, the bank must make payment. If there is not sufficient money in the account, the bank need not make payment unless it has agreed an overdraft facility. It is very easy to overlook bank charges, standing orders, direct debits and even cheque payments, so particular care is needed when you know the account is approaching zero or an agreed overdraft limit.

There are two types of overdraft: authorized, and unauthorised. An **authorized overdraft** has been agreed with the bank. It will be for a fixed amount and will usually have a time limit. The bank may change an **arrangement fee** for agreeing an overdraft facility. Having a facility does not require you to use it (though if you do not, you may have difficulty renewing it). If you do not use it, you pay no interest on the facility. The bank will want to know why you need an overdraft and will expect it to be to meet a temporary need or to smooth out large fluctuations between income and expenditure cycles. Otherwise a bank, obviously, expects the church to live within its means. Internet banking makes it much easier to keep an eye on the state of a bank account.

An **unauthorized overdraft** is when a person exceeds a limit without authority. A bank is not obliged to let anyone have an unauthorized overdraft and may simply dishonour the cheque. Many modern accounts now allow for a small unauthorized overdraft. The charges for an unauthorized overdraft are exorbitant. You are first hit with a penalty charge, which could be £30, and the interest rate is much higher than for an authorized overdraft. Rates above 25% are common. Some banks charge extra for every cheque issued during a period of unauthorized overdraft. In pure financial terms, it is *always* better to arrange a loan or delay paying a bill rather than incur an unauthorized overdraft.

An overdraft is always repayable on demand. This means that the bank may at any time demand that the money is immediately repaid. If it is not, the authorized overdraft becomes an unauthorized one. Banks do not do this as a matter of practice, and advice from the British Bankers' Association implies this will only happen if your circumstances change to justify such action. However, you must appreciate that any form of overdraft puts you at the mercy of the bank to some extent, and their prime interest is to their shareholders, not to their customers.

Bank loans

A bank loan is an arrangement where the bank provides funds for a fixed period (the **loan term**) which you repay with interest. The amount you borrow is called the **capital** (or principal) to which is added **interest** and charges.

There are many forms of bank loan. Most forms require you to repay a portion of the capital with interest in regular instalments until the loan is cleared. It is also possible to borrow money so that a single payment is made at the end of the loan term. Another possibility is to pay interest only in instalments, and then repay just the capital.

The interest is calculated as either a **fixed rate** or **variable rate**. A fixed rate means that the rate of interest does not change during the loan period. A variable rate fluctuates, usually in accordance with the base rate set by the Bank of England.

Interest rates

Interest is a charge for the use of someone else's money. Sometimes Christians see interest charges as being immoral, though it is difficult to see the objection to making a charge for borrowing the property of cash but no objection to a charge for hiring a church hall.

First – some theology

The Old Testament principle was basically that it was acceptable to charge interest as part of a commercial enterprise but not when relieving misfortune. Someone who provides capital for an enterprise is contributing to its success and it is therefore equitable that such a contributor should share in the fruits of its success. This remains the basis for modern shareholdings in companies. Jesus' parable of the talents shows that there is no objection to investment: 'You ought to have put my money on deposit, and on my return I should have got it back with interest' (Matthew 25.27).

For the relief of misfortune, the law said: 'If you advance money to any poor man amongst my people, you are not to act like a moneylender; you must not exact interest from him' (Exodus 22.25). It is reasonable to expect the loan to be repaid when the man is restored to prosperity, but not for him to pay more. This remains the basis in some areas, such as for budgeting loans under the Social Fund run by the state (if you can get one), but generally this principle has sadly now been lost in British society.

The Authorized Version of the Bible uses the word 'usury', but its meaning there is not the modern one of extortionate interest:

it is the old meaning of an interest charge at any rate for the relief of poverty.

In making a comparison between Old Testament and contemporary British practices, it should also be noted that an Old Testament loan could be secured by property, failing which the debtor could be sold into slavery. To mitigate these consequences, every seventh year debts were forgiven (Deuteronomy 15.1). They could also be mitigated in the year of Jubilee. There is evidence that these laws were not always followed.

Modern English law has lost the concept of irresponsible indebtedness being a crime. Consumer debt exceeded £1.5 trillion in June 2009. However, the idea of seizing property to repay debts and then forgiving the balance is the basis of modern bankruptcy law.

Second – some mathematics

The simplest form of interest is appropriately called **simple interest**. Interest is added to the principal only. If you borrow £100 at 6% per year, you owe £106 after one year, £112 after two, £118 after three, and so on. Simple interest is used in a few narrow areas, such as for certificates of tax deposit and on court judgements.

In the example above, you owe £106 after one year but only pay interest on £100. In other words, you are now borrowing another £6 interest free. For this reason, it is far more common to use **compound interest**. In year two, you pay 6% interest on £106, which brings the total to £112.36, and so on.

A comparison between the two systems produces these figures:

	Simple interest	Compound interest
Year 0	100.00	100.00
Year 1	106.00	106.00
Year 2	112.00	112.36
Year 3	118.00	119.10
Year 4	124.00	126.25

It can be seen that compound interest produces higher figures, but after four years it is only 1% higher than simple interest. The difference becomes significant over long periods of time:

	Simple interest	*Compound interest*
Year 10	160	179.08
Year 20	220	320.71
Year 30	280	574.35
Year 40	340	1,028.57
Year 50	400	1,842.02
Year 100	700	33,930.21

One curiosity is that simple interest produces higher figures over periods of less than one year. Over three months a loan of £100 at 6% interest produces a simple interest charge of £1.50, but only £1.47 compound interest.

For budgeting and mental arithmetic purposes, there is a simple **rule of 72**. This states that if you divide 72 by the interest rate, the answer is the number of years for the principal to double in value. So for 6%, £100 will have become £200 after twelve years; at 8% it will double after nine years. Although this is obviously an approximation, it is a remarkably accurate one.

For loans and investments, two different rates are quoted: actual rate, and annual percentage rate (APR).

You use the actual rate for calculations and APR for comparisons. The reason for having APR is because what appears to be the same actual rate can lead to significantly different costs depending on how frequently payments are made, whether interest is charged in advance or arrears, and how frequently the principal is adjusted to reflect payments.

4

Budgeting and Expenses

Budgets and forecasts

A **forecast** is what the treasurer expects to happen. It is a hope or expectation. A **budget** is a management decision of what should happen. It is an order.

The budget should be drawn up first, ideally before the start of the year. This is a management decision and must be made by the church council, and not the treasurer acting alone. The budget reflects the priorities and convictions of the church. It should be seen as a mission statement rather than just a routine financial document.

Types of budget

There are two common types of budget: annual budget, and zero-based budget (ZBB).

The **annual budget** is usually calculated by adjusting previous years' figures in the light of experience. The laziest form of annual budget is simply to take last year's figures and increase them by an amount to represent inflation.

The **zero-based budget** is so called because all items of expenditure start at zero, and every penny must be justified afresh each year. This is seen as the more radical and dynamic approach, but the difference between the two can be nominal. A ZBB may agree a particular figure on being last year's figure plus a bit to represent inflation.

For a budget to have any purpose, there must be a budget holder for every item of discretionary expenditure. A church has some items of expenditure over which it has little control, such as insurance and electricity. For all other items, there should be a designated individual whose job it is to keep within that spending limit. If the budget holder wishes to exceed his limit, the matter must be referred to the church council.

A budget does not just cover expenditure, but must cover income also. In commercial organizations, this can be seen as an instruction to the sales department on how much they are expected to generate in sales. In a non-commercial organization, it can be seen as an aim. A church cannot order its members to give more money, but it can exhort them to do so.

There is another type of budget known as the **flexible budget**. This is appropriate when income and expenditure are closely related, such as if selling more goods means buying more material. It is not likely to be that relevant for a church.

Some theology

It is usually at this point in the proceedings that someone will quote the following gospel passage:

> No one can serve two masters; for either he will hate the first and love the second, or he will be devoted to the first and despise the second. You cannot serve God and Money.
>
> This is why I tell you not to be anxious about food and drink to keep you alive and about clothes to cover your body. Surely life is more than food, the body more than clothes. Look at the birds in the sky; they do not sow and reap and store in barns, yet your heavenly Father feeds them. Are you not worth more than the birds? Can anxious thought add a single day to your life? And why be anxious about clothes? Consider how the lilies grow in the fields; they do not work; they do not spin; yet I tell you, even Solomon in all his splendour was not attired like one of them.
>
> If that is how God clothes the grass in the fields, which is there today and tomorrow is thrown on the stove, will he not all the more clothe you? How little faith you have! Do not ask anxiously, 'What are we to drink? What shall we wear?' These are the things that occupy the minds of the heathen, but your heavenly Father knows that you need them all. Set your mind on God's kingdom and his justice before everything else, and all the rest will come to you as well. So do not be anxious about tomorrow; tomorrow will look after itself. Each day has troubles enough of its own. (Matthew 6.24–34)

At first sight this well-known passage seems to imply that any form of budgeting or financial planning is intrinsically wrong. However, that is a consequence of not studying scripture carefully and not considering the totality of scripture. This passage is concerned about trusting God and not being anxious. It is a mistake to see this as being an injunction for laziness or against prudent planning. This is where other scripture needs to be considered also. The need to work is reflected in a passage such as:

> Already during our stay with you we laid down this rule: anyone who will not work shall not eat. We mention this because we hear that some of you are idling their time away, minding everyone's business but their own. We instruct and urge such people in the name of the Lord Jesus Christ to settle down to work and earn a living. (2 Thessalonians 3.10–12).

As for financial planning, the parable of the talents (Matthew 25.14–30) is a clear example. The man who simply hid his master's bag of gold in the ground rather than used it to generate more capital is told, 'You ought to have put my money on deposit, and on my return I should have got it back with interest' (v. 27).

There is plenty of scripture commending us to be wise and prudent, and to plan. There is also plenty of reference to eternal life as future treasure, such as 1 Timothy 6.19. Treasure itself is not evil. Solomon was blessed with treasure. It is the *love of money* that is the root of all evil (1 Timothy 6.10), not money itself.

In church circles, there is often concern that the church is finance-driven rather than vision-led. Provided the accountants are Christian, the church is often better run when finance-driven. The answer is in a balanced approach of making reasonable plans while not becoming anxious: care without worry.

Budget holders

Every budget holder must accept responsibility for their budget. There must be financial discipline in the expenditure of resources entrusted to God's work.

Each budget holder should consider these matters:

- a budget is a maximum amount to be spent. It should not be spent just because you have it to spend

- deduct from your budget those items over which you have no real control or amounts which you know must be incurred
- divide the balance by 12 to give a monthly figure of free funds to spend as you see fit
- keep a running total to see how your spending compares with the budget
- if it becomes clear that you cannot reasonably keep within your budget, discuss the matter with the church council before you overspend.

This simple process can be accommodated in a notebook or on a back page of a diary. There is no need for the budget holder to keep detailed records – the treasurer does that. The budget holder is simply monitoring expenditure entrusted to his care.

This is where some honesty between church members is essential. Not everyone is good with handling money. The fact that someone is an excellent secretary, preacher, teacher, youth worker, organist, magazine editor, caretaker, coffee maker, flower arranger or whatever does not always mean that they are excellent in handling funds. The treasurer will in effect be monitoring the budget holders by the forecast, but it may be necessary to provide some help at an earlier stage if a budget holder is having difficulty in coping.

Always take a firm line with unauthorized expenditure. The doors of the church may be open to all, but the offices of the church are only open to those who demonstrate fitness to occupy them. If someone orders goods without authority, take a firm line, which may mean sending the goods back and telling the supplier who has authority to order further goods. This may be awkward at the time, but will prevent much more serious problems later.

It should be possible to plot expenditure against budget as the year progresses. This will show when a category of expenditure looks likely to exceed its budget. This should be brought back to the church council, or other body which set the budget, for investigation. A breach of budget means:

- that the budget was not realistically set in the first place;
- that something unexpected happened;
- the budget holder did not exercise sufficient discipline; or
- a combination of these three.

Whatever the reason, it needs investigation and action.

Forecast

The forecast has two elements:

- monitoring progress during the year so far
- projecting figures for the rest of the year.

The progress simply records how much has already been received and spent against each budget item so far. It is simple factual reporting.

The projected figures simply multiply that for the rest of the year. So if someone has spent £360 in three months, the twelve-month figure can be forecast as £1,440, unless you know that some payments are seasonal, so a higher or lower figure is appropriate. If the person's budget is £1,000, it is already clear that the person is overspending. This is a policy matter for the church council or finance committee to consider. It may be that the budget holder stocked up in the early part of the year and only needs to spend about £60 a month for the remainder. It may be that the church council recognizes that the budget was set too low and needs to be increased. There are many conclusions that may be derived, but what matters is that the treasurer produces the forecast to allow such a discussion to take place.

Inflation

A church treasurer needs to understand inflation, particularly when presenting budgets and forecasts, and answering questions at meetings of church members.

Money does not hold its value. Inflation means that £1 today is usually worth less than £1 yesterday. It is possible for the opposite to happen, and for there to be deflation when currency gains in value. This happened during the depression of the early 1930s and last happened in March 1960 when 'inflation' was −0.5%.

In the UK, inflation has been around 5% or less every month since June 1992, but historically it has been much higher. Just two years earlier, in 1990, inflation rates were above 10%. In August 1975, inflation reached 26.9%. It is always possible for such high rates to return, but even low rates can have a significant impact over long periods.

Several points must be understood about inflation.

1. Inflation relates to consumer spending only, not to wages

Inflation is calculated by the Office for National Statistics by reference to various indices. From 10 December 2003, the official index is the consumer price index (CPI), previously known as the harmonized index of consumer prices (HICP – the name was changed because it was referred to as 'hiccup'). This was preceded by the retail prices index (RPI) from 1947, which in turn succeeded the cost of living index introduced in 1914. CPI is the base used by all European Union countries and many other countries, allowing international comparisons to be made.

All of these methods take a 'basket of goods' which reflects typical consumer spending. The content of this basket changes in accordance with changes in spending patterns. Recent items added include frozen chicken nuggets, hamsters, laptop computers, cash machine charges and chiropractor fees. Among items excluded were razor blades, cat food, writing paper, children's slippers and food processors. In 1914, the list included corsets and wig powder.

CPI differs from RPI in that it:

- includes all consumer spending whereas RPI excludes the wealthiest and poorest 4%
- excludes mortgages and council tax
- includes more services in addition to goods
- uses different mathematics (such as geometric mean) to give smoother changes.

Since its introduction, CPI has produced lower rates of inflation than RPI. For example, in the year to September 2011, CPI recorded 5.2% inflation against 5.6% for RPI.

In reality, there are not just one or two indices, but dozens of them reflecting different combinations of goods.

The significance for the treasurer is that these well-publicized measures of inflation are of little relation to the church, as a church spends little of its income on consumer goods like potatoes and shirts. Most church expenditure is on wages.

It is quite normal for wages to rise by two percentage points more than consumer goods. This leads to greater prosperity, which is why each generation is better off than the previous generation.

However since the economic crisis started from 2008, wages

have tended to increase by less than inflation. For most of 2011, wage inflation was around 2.3%.

This means that a person who earned and spent £100 one year ago, will now (on average) earn £102.30 but need to spend £105.20 to buy the same items. At the time of writing, it is not clear how long this situation will last.

2. Investment income creates a gearing effect

The Church of England has huge historic resources administered for it by the Church Commissioners. Other churches can have significant endowments and other historic resources.

The existence of any form of investment creates a gearing effect which magnifies the effect of inflation. Suppose a church has income and expenditure of £100,000, of which £40,000 comes from interest on a deposit of £1.5 million left by a widow. It wishes to increase its expenditure by 5% to £105,000. If the interest remains the same, this means that the giving must increase from £70,000 to £75,000, which is 7% more. This means that a 5% increase in spending needs a 7% increase in giving.

Suppose the church does not raise any of the extra £5,000 and so takes it from the deposit. This creates a double gearing effect as it reduces the interest charge in future years. In the example above, this would reduce the investment income to £39,867. For next year, a 5% increase in spending would need a 7.3% increase in giving.

3. It measures increases in prices not loss of value

If inflation is 5% that means that average goods which cost £100 one year ago now cost £105. It does not mean that £100 now is only worth £95 then. It means that £100 is worth £100 × 100/105, which is £95.24. Over one year, the difference is small, but over many years this difference becomes much greater. We return to this subject when we look at discounted cashflow.

5

Legal requirements

The law

To do any job properly, you must know the legal context in which you operate.

The church is a charity. Its accounts therefore must comply the accounting requirements of charity law. In England and Wales, this is in the Charities Act 1993, as amended by Charities Act 2006.

Accounts should comply with the statement of recommended practice (SORP) for charity accounting issued by the Charity Commissioners. The latest version was issued in March 2005, replacing one in 2000 (which was amended in 2002 and 2003), which itself replaced a SORP issued in 1995. The 2005 SORP applies for accounting periods which start on or after 1 April 2005.

Many of the changes in the 2005 SORP are of explanation and clarification, rather than making substantive changes to the accounting requirements.

These regulations are designed to ensure public confidence in those who collect money for the common good.

In general, charities must submit annual accounts to the Charity Commissioners. Most church denominations are exempt from the requirement to submit accounts, but must keep accounts on the same basis as if accounts were submitted. Some church groups may not be exempt, and some church bodies may not be within the scope of the exemption. In addition, any church may choose to submit accounts voluntarily if it really wishes, though there is no reason why a church would so wish.

There are also accounting regulations issued by the Accounting Standards Board (ASB). Although these are generally written for commercial businesses, some of them do contain provisions which are relevant to churches.

Each denomination has its own rules. In the Church of England, some of these rules have the force of law. They include the Church Accounting Regulations 1997 as amended in 2001.

On top of all this law and regulation, there is also much which is simply regarded as good practice. This includes having two people count the collection, and banking the collection promptly.

Size of church

Charity accounts may be prepared differently according to the amount of money handled by the church.

Larger churches must prepare accounts on the accruals basis. Smaller churches *may* either also use the accruals basis, or may use the simpler receipts and payments basis.

Certain grant-making bodies require accruals accounts whatever the size of the church. So if you are planning to make a request for a grant, you may need to use accruals accounting anyway.

For England and Wales, accruals accounts must be prepared if the income exceeds £250,000. This applies to accounts for periods that end after 31 March 2009.

For previous periods, the figure is £100,000 unless *expenditure* exceeded £250,000. That limit was introduced in 1997.

The definition of what constitutes income is defined in Charities Act 1993 s97. This includes gross income from all sources, including from special trusts.

Note that this includes *income* from all sources. This means that if a church sells books or gifts, or hires its hall, all such income must be included. So if a church has £200,000 worth of voluntary giving, and £30,000 income from £60,000 worth of sales, it must prepare accrual accounts, as its income is £260,000.

For these purposes, income includes receipts into a restricted fund.

Further advice on determining gross income is given later in this chapter.

However the threshold only applies to new income. So a church which has income of £200,000 but draws another £70,000 from reserves to spend £270,000 is below the threshold. The £70,000 withdrawn is not new income,

In contrast the £250,000 limit applies to income *or expenditure*. Also, this limit is not just considered for the current year, but also for either of the previous two years. The limit applies to most church income and expenditure, not just routine income or expenditure. So if a church has a particularly large sum of income or expenditure one year, perhaps to buy an organ or replace the roof, that could mean the church is 'over £250,000' for that year and the following two years, even if the income and expenditure falls below £250,000 in those following years.

If a church's income exceeds £250,000 one year and then falls below this threshold the next year, it may legally go back to producing receipts and payments accounts. However this is not good accounting practice for two reasons. First, one function of accounting is to allow comparison between consecutive years to see how items of income and expenditure have changed, and second, in the year of changeover some items will be included twice and others not at all.

An example of the second point is if a church receives an electricity bill in one year when it produces receipts and payments accounts, and pays it in the next year when it produces accrual accounts. The bill will not be included in either accounts. It does not appear in the former year as the bill was not paid then. It does not appear in the latter year's accounts as it accrued in the previous year.

Charity accounting rules have a further provision that charities with income of less than £10,000 are not required to submit accounts at all, but must still keep accounts. This is a regulation which the Church of England and most other denominations specifically disapply, so in practice all churches must prepare accounts.

Different countries

In **Scotland**, the relevant law is now Charities and Finance Investment (Scotland) Act 2005. This establishes the Office of the Scottish Charity Regulator (OSCR).

There is no Scottish equivalent to an excepted charity, so every Scottish church must register with the regulator. There are some administrative provisions that relax some of the law's provisions for designated religious charities.

Every church and charity must submit an annual return to the regulator with an annual report and financial statements.

A Scottish church or charity must use accruals accounting if income exceeds £100,000 a year. Below this figure they may prepare receipts and payments accounts.

A church or charity with income above £25,000 must also produce a 'monitoring return'. This is a nine-page document that must be submitted to OSCR.

The accounts must be audited by a qualified accountant authorised to audit company accounts if either:

- gross income exceeds £500,000 or more, or
- aggregate value of assets exceeds £2.8 million *and* gross income exceeds £100,000.

The accounts and returns are monitored and validated. Churches and charities that fail to submit correct documents will be asked to re-submit them. If problems persist, the charity could be removed from the register.

It should also be noted that Scotland has its own Parliament and system of law. There are many other significant differences between English and Scottish law.

In **Northern Ireland,** churches and other charities will come within the scope of the Charities Act (Northern Ireland) 2008. At the time of writing, this Act has not been brought fully into force.

This Act will largely mirror English law.

Until then, the only legal requirement is Charities Act (Northern Ireland) 1964. This requires that charities prepare proper records and keep them for seven years. There is no set threshold on when accruals accounts must be used. A charity registers only with HMRC (Inland Revenue before 18 April 2005).

The **Republic of Ireland** is not part of the UK but follows many of the same legal principles.

Charities will be regulated by Charities Act 2009 passed by the Houses of the Oireachtas and not yet fully in force when this book was published.

This Act requires charities to keep 'proper books of account' and to prepare annual audited statements.

Until then, churches and charities do not register with anyone other than the Revenue Commissioners under Irish Income Tax Act 1967. UK accounting standards have traditionally been adopted in the Republic. The 2000 Charities SORP was said to apply to the Republic, but the 2005 version is only encouraged.

How the size is determined

In deciding whether the £100,000 or £250,000 threshold has been crossed, it is necessary to understand what figures are included.

Only amounts of money paid to or by the church are included. Money paid by someone else is not included even if it is for the benefit of the church. So a vicar's stipend is not included in church expenditure because it is paid centrally and not by the church.

Also, **non-monetary items** received or given away are not included. If someone gives the church a piano, its value is not included as income. If the church gives away some old hymn books, that is not included as expenditure.

The following items are *not* included as income:

- the amount of any loan paid to the PCC;
- repayment of any loan made by the PCC to someone else;
- the proceeds from selling any investments;
- the proceeds from selling a 'functional fixed asset' such as the church hall or curate's house;
- interest-only endowments.

For the last item, it is possible for someone to give an **endowment** to a church on the basis that the church may spend the interest but not the capital sum of an endowment. In such a case, the interest is included as income but the capital sum is not. If someone donates £100,000 to a church in this way, from which the church receives £5,000 interest in the year, only the £5,000 is included as income. Endowments are explained on page 11.

Amounts received from **insurance claims** may also be excluded in practice, as these are intended simply to replace what the church already had and restore it to its same financial position.

The following items are *not* included as expenditure:

- any loan made by the PCC to someone else;
- repayment of a loan made by the PCC;
- purchase of investments;
- purchase of a 'functional fixed asset';
- any loss on the sale of a functional fixed asset; and
- any transfer of funds to or from an endowment account or high-interest account, or to or from any other account controlled by the same church.

A functional fixed asset must be to further the mission of the church.

Income and expenditure must not be netted off. For example if the church holds a fete which generates £5,000 in income and incurs £2,000 in expenditure, the whole £5,000 must be included as income and the whole £2,000 as expenditure. It is not acceptable to net the figures off and include just £3,000 net income. Similar provisions apply to fetes, magazines, sweepstakes and concerts.

A church may not know whether it will cross the threshold. In such cases, the church is advised to prepare its accounts on the basis of the higher figure. There is no penalty for preparing accounts on a stricter basis than the law requires. However a church cannot avoid its duty to prepare accounts on a particular basis because it did not expect to cross the threshold. This can mean that unexpected income during the year could require the treasurer to change the basis of preparing the accounts.

So what is the accruals basis?

The accruals basis attempts to match income and expenditure to the same period. The accruals basis looks at when the entitlement to receive money or the liability to pay money arose, rather than when the money was actually received or paid.

In contrast, the receipts and payments method (also known as 'cash accounting') simply lists income received and expenditure incurred during the year, regardless of to what period it refers.

Suppose on 1 October, you pay an insurance premium of £2,000 for the year. Under the receipts and payments method, you include the £2,000 as expenditure for that year because that is when you paid it. Under the accruals basis, you would only include £500 for the three months to the year-end on 31 December. For the first nine months, you include three-quarters of the premium paid in the previous year, which may be a different amount.

What must be clearly understood is that the day-to-day record keeping is exactly the same whichever basis you use. The accruals basis simply requires you to make some extra adjustments at the end of the year.

Those adjustments relate to any income or expenditure which is related to a period of time. Examples include:

- insurance premiums;
- rent paid or received;
- wages and salaries;
- income from investments;
- telephone bills;
- hire and lease payments;
- loan repayments.

The adjustment may be an addition to or subtraction from either income or expenditure.

For example, an addition to income is made when income was received in a previous year for the current year, such as when someone renting church property paid three months' rent in advance in December.

A subtraction from expenditure is made when the figure covers a future period, such as paying three months' telephone line rental in advance in December.

Telephone bills often include one figure for the line rental payable in advance, and another figure for calls paid in arrears. These elements of the bill must be separately accounted for. This is best illustrated by an example considering telephone bills submitted on 1 December 2011 and 1 February 2012 thus:

Item	1 December 2011	1 February 2012
Line rental	£60	£66
Calls	£90	£72
Total	£150	£138

In 2011, you include:

£20 line rental (one third of £60)
£90 calls on 1 December 2011 bill
£24 calls (one third of February 2012 bill)
£134 included in 2011 accounts

In 2012, you include:

£40 line rental (prepaid on 1 December 2011 bill)
£66 line rental on 1 February 2012 bill
£48 calls on 1 February 2012 (for January and February)
£154 included in 2012 accounts

Note that we have still accounted for the whole £288 on these two telephone bills whichever basis we use. The difference is that, under the accruals basis, we adjust the figures to the years to which they relate.

Whatever figures are added or subtracted at the end of the year must be reversed for the following year. If you reduced the insurance premium by £1,000 for the current year, you must add £1,000 to insurance premium for the next year.

It can be seen that the accruals basis can delay preparing the accounts for the year. Under the receipts and payments method, on 1 January you can prepare your accounts for the year to 31 December. For the accruals basis, you must wait until some later bills arrive. There is no obligation to wait unduly long. If after two months, a bill for the previous year has not been received, it is acceptable for the treasurer to estimate the bill and accrue the proportion of that estimate.

Other provisions for accruals accounting

Once a church comes within the scope of accruals accounting, not only must the church use the accruals method of accounting, but it must also:

- produce a balance sheet;
- comply with accounting standards;
- produce accounts that are 'true and fair';
- make full disclosures, particularly in notes to the accounts.

Which funds are included?

The treasurer will often find that the church does not just have one account, but has several accounts. The treasurer may also find that there are other funds held by people within the church or by organisations connected to the church. There may be funds held separately by Scouts, magazine editor, choir, flower arrangers, caterers, social committee and others.

The treasurer must establish whether each fund is to be included as church funds. This determines not only whether the appropriate threshold has been crossed, but whether the income and expenditure of that fund must be added to the church's other income and expenditure. If funds are raised using the church's charitable status to recover income tax, the funds belong to the church.

The test is whether the funds are owned or controlled by the church. If the body is outside the control of the church, their funds are not consolidated. This will apply to Scouts and other bodies who simply hire the church hall. The church accounts include only the amount the scouts or other body pay the church for using its facilities.

If the body is controlled by the church and the funds ultimately belong to the church, they are included. This will usually be the case for funds held by the magazine editor and flower arrangers. If such people do hold funds, they must understand that they are accountable to you as treasurer for those funds, and must keep a record of income and expenditure. It is not acceptable for someone to say that they have made £200 profit from selling coffee after the service but not know how much people paid for the coffee and how much was spent buying the ingredients. A fund may not be excluded just because the treasurer has difficulty getting his hands on it, nor because there are restrictions on how it may be spent.

Sometimes people may contribute money for a specific purpose, such as to buy flowers or give choirboys an outing. Such money must be included as church income and expenditure. In some cases, the involvement of the treasurer may be seen as an intrusion into what is 'none of his business'. Sometimes tact may be needed to obtain the figures. A treasurer who is finding difficulties should draw the problem to the attention of the minister or church council.

Where a church organises a collection for another body, funds collected do not belong to the church. An example is the annual house-to-house collection for Christian Aid. If the church banks money and the treasurer issues a church cheque to the charity, the church is acting as a trust for the charity. Such income is not included in the SOFA but must be mentioned in the notes to the accounts.

Where fees are collected to be paid to church officers, such as organist, bellringers and flower-arranger at a wedding or funeral, those funds again do not belong to the church.

Sometimes a bowl may be placed at a funeral service inviting donations. It must be clear at the outset if these donations are for the church's general funds or if they are for a charity nominated by the deceased or his family. If the latter, the church is acting as agent for that charity and those funds are not accounted for as church funds.

If the funds do not ultimately belong to the church, they are not included. So if members of the choir pool their funds to pay for an outing, or members of a house group pool funds to pay for a dinner, that fund is not included. The money does not legally belong to the church.

Whenever there is a fund of money in the church, there must never be the slightest doubt as to:

- who owns the money;
- the purpose for which the money may be spent; and
- who decides how to spend the money.

There can be great bitterness between church members if this rule is not followed, even if the amount is small.

A fund is included if the answer to any of these questions is yes:

- is it owned by a body (known as a 'special trust') which is accountable to the church rather than the general public?
- is it owned by a body controlled by the church?
- is it owned by a body controlled by people on behalf of the church?

Note that if the answer is no, the fund is a separate body, and will usually be required to register with the Charity Commissioners and submit its own accounts.

Funds held by an organisation which is accountable to a **parent body**, such as the Mothers Union, are not included as church funds.

A **'friends' group** may exists to raise funds for the church or for some specific purpose of the church. If the friends group is separately registered as a charity, the church accounts only includes donations received from it, but must mention the existence of the charity. Otherwise, the friends' funds must be included as church funds.

A minister may operate a **discretionary fund**, such as to assist individuals with particular problems. The payment of money to the minister is included as church expenditure in the year that the church paid the money. Thereafter the fund is not included as church funds. The minister is only obliged to report payments to the extent required by the church when making the fund available. As such payments are usually confidential, it is good practice for the minister to account to just one, or perhaps two, other people. This may be the treasurer, churchwarden, auditor or examiner, or whoever else the church appoints. The whole point of producing charity accounts at all is to assure the public that the funds are being properly administered. Having one other person knowing the recipients, amounts and balance gives the minister the same protection and helps prevent any embarrassment later.

Trusts are explained in more detail in Chapter 14, but two aspects of them may be noted here. First, any trust fund which is controlled by another body, such as a Diocesan Board of Education, is not included in the church accounts. Second, bequests from wills are often held in a separate account to be spent as the vicar and churchwardens (not the church council) may decide. Such funds are also not included in the church accounts, but their existence should be noted on the accounts.

Sometimes another officer of the church may arrange a fete, concert, exhibition or similar which involves money. The treasurer must ensure that this money is promptly accounted for, and should not be fobbed off. A person who cannot look after the income and expenditure of a fete or concert should not be allowed to do so.

Who is the church?

Sometimes not only is there the problem of identifying which funds belong to the church, there can be a problem in identifying who or what is 'the church'.

For a single parish church or a single Methodist chapel, the answer is usually obvious. However there are now many arrangements of daughter churches, church plants, shared buildings, local ecumenical projects, team ministries, united benefices, pluralities and similar where the answer is less obvious.

The basic rule is that accounts must be prepared for a **legal entity**.

In the Church of England, the legal entity is the parochial church council (PCC). The PCC controls funds for its daughter church or a church plant, so their accounts must be included.

For **united benefices** and pluralities, each parish in the benefice or plurality is a legal entity and so must produce its own accounts.

A **team** may comprise separate parishes, or be one parish with separate district church councils (DCCs). Again the accounts must be prepared for the parish. Although some PCC responsibilities may be passed to DCCs, financial responsibilities are specifically excluded. The PCC legally must prepare a single set of accounts which covers the whole team.

This can be a sensitive issue when rural parishes have been merged and former PCCs are relegated to the status of DCC. Not preparing separate accounts can be seen as a loss of identity which can engender strong feelings. However the loss of separate accounting is not itself the cause of the problem but just a consequence of the fact that the parishes merged. Such concerns should be addressed at the time of the merger and not be a cause of subsequent obstruction to treasurers.

A **local ecumenical project** (LEP) or shared building typically involves two or more churches, often of different denominations, working together. Each is a legal entity and must therefore produce its own accounts. The agreement for the LEP or sharing should specify what costs and what share of common costs are the responsibility of each church. Only those costs should be included in the accounts of each church.

All accounting regulations specify the **minimum reporting** standard. Any church, or indeed any company or anyone else, is free to prepare additional accounts and voluntarily offer whatever additional information it wishes. So DCCs may prepare individual accounts for themselves, and teams of parishes may prepare consolidated accounts. However such additional accounts have no legal status, have no requirement to be audited or examined, and are no substitute for the accounts which must be prepared by law.

Legal form

Charity law simply determines the status of an organisation; it does not prescribe any legal form. So a charity must adopt a form by one of six different routes:

- unincorporated association;
- trust;
- limited company;
- industrial and provident society;
- Royal Charter; or
- corporation created by statute.

The first two of these give no protection to the charity's founders, so they can personally be sued for any loss sustained by the charity. Although a trust can incorporate under Charities Act 1993 s50, that does not give the trustees limited liability.

Incorporation by Royal Charter is costly and discretionary; only 161 charities have been so chartered since 1518.

Most charities opt to be a limited company. The members of the company (those who own the company) limit their liability to an amount they either contribute by buying shares or, more commonly for charities, agree to pay should the company be wound up. The latter type of company is known as a company limited by guarantee. The amount the members agree to contribute is usually a nominal sum, typically £1 each.

The problem with charities which are limited companies is that they must comply with two sets of regulations: returns to the Charity Commission, and returns to Companies House. There are also unresolved conflicts between charity law and company law.

To address this problem, the various draft charities bills propose the creation of a new body called the Charitable Incorporated Organisation (CIO). This would provide a single means of incorporating a charity with limited company for members.

This will provide a convenient legal form for those churches which must register with the Charity Commission. It will also be a convenient form for charities run by other churches.

6

Accounting

Introduction

This section provides an outline guide to some basic accounting principles.

A church treasurer does not need to be qualified as an accountant. However, some basic principles of accounting should be understood. This is particularly important if your turnover is above £250,000 a year and you must prepare accounts under the accruals basis. Even if your turnover is below £250,000, some understanding of basic accounting principles is always useful.

Monetarism

Accounting is only concerned with those items to which a monetary value can readily be atttributed. Clearly there is great value in historic buildings, graveyards, a happy congregation, good preaching and many other attributes, but no monetary value can be readily attributed to them.

Note that the value shown in the accounts is the value to the church. It is not the amount for which an asset could be sold, nor is it the cost of a replacement.

Assets and liabilities

An asset is:

- cash
- something that will become cash
- something worth cash.

Cash can be in the forms of banknotes and coins, or as a deposit at a bank.

Something that will be a cash is a debtor (someone who owes you money) and whom we assume will pay you. Also, a prepayment is an asset. This is when you pay for something before you use it, such as paying rent in advance.

Items worth cash are further distinguished between **current assets** and **fixed assets**. The former are assets you intend to consume within a year, such as stationery, stamps and any stock you hold to sell. Fixed assets are intended to last for more than one year. They are the property used to maintain the organization, such as buildings, furniture and vehicles.

A **liability** is the opposite of an asset. It is represented by an overdraft at the bank, a creditor (someone to whom you owe money) or an accrual (incurring a liability which has yet to be charged to you, such as making telephone calls which have yet to be billed).

Every asset and liability is an **account** in the financial records. There are some additional accounts which are neither assets nor liabilities.

Profit, loss, surplus and deficit

Only a commercial business can make a profit or a loss. For a non-commercial entity, such as a church, the equivalent terms are surplus or deficit.

A **profit** is the reason a commercial business exists. A business which makes a **loss** is a business which is failing. It is as simple as that. A business may make a loss in the short term such as when it is starting or just after a reorganization, but if it does not make a profit overall it is a failing business.

A church is different in that no one runs it to make a profit; at least no one should do. It seeks to stay solvent and be able to meet its bills as they fall due. Its overall aim is not to make a profit but to break even. A **surplus** simply means that it received more money than it needed in that period. A **deficit** does not mean that the church is failing financially; a series of surpluses and deficits is quite acceptable. Persistent deficits indicate a problem, but occasional deficits do not.

Double-entry book-keeping

Almost all accounting systems use double-entry book-keeping, although this may not always be obvious.

Double-entry book-keeping is based on the principle that every financial transaction affects two accounts. If you cash a cheque, you have more money in cash but less money in the bank. If you buy stationery on account, you have more stationery but also have more owed to creditors. When you pay the bill, you reduce the amount of money you have in the bank, but also reduce the money owed to creditors.

This led to the invention of double-entry book-keeping in Genoa, Italy, in 1340. Transactions were recorded using two columns of figures headed *dare* (to give) and *avere* (to receive). This is why the word 'debit' is abbreviated to 'Dr'. A book recording these transactions is known as a **journal**. A modern bank statement looks remarkably similar to a journal; change the headings 'Paid out' and 'Paid in' to 'Credit' and 'Debit' and you have a journal (albeit with the columns the wrong way round).

If you keep petty cash, you probably have a little cash book kept in the box, where left-hand pages record cash 'in' and the right-hand pages record cash 'out'. Change the words 'in' and 'out' to 'debit' and 'credit' and you have a cash journal.

Double-entry was adopted by Venetian traders in the fifteenth century and soon spread to the rest of the world.

Many people coming fresh to book-keeping are confused by the fact that money received is regarded as a debit and not a credit. In book-keeping, the word 'credit' means the exact opposite to normal parlance. If we pay money into our bank, we say we have *credited* our bank account whereas in book-keeping terms we have *debited* our bank account. This is because the bank statement is produced from the bank's perspective, not yours. If XYZ owes you £100, XYZ is your debtor, and you are XYZ's creditor. From the bank's perspective, the money has been credited as it is money that it must pay you.

The next confusion for book-keeping students is whether part of a transaction should be a debit or a credit. If you go back to thinking of cash and other assets as a debit, it is often possible to work it out from first principles. It can be summarized by Table 1.

Table 1. Debits and credits

	Increase	Decrease
Asset	Debit	Credit
Liability	Credit	Debit

In any transaction, the total of all debits must equal the total of all credits.

Let us consider the transactions we mentioned earlier:

- We cash a cheque for £100:
    debit cash by £100, credit bank by £100.
- We buy £50 worth of stationery on account:
    debit stationery by £50; credit creditors by £50
- We pay the stationery bill of £50:
    debit creditors by £50; credit bank by £50.

Sometimes there may be more than one debit or more than one credit. This is acceptable, provided the total debits equals the total credits. Suppose our stationery supply sold us a desk for £300 and stationery for £60. The double entries for that supply are:

- Debit furniture £300; debit stationery £60; credit creditors £360.

When any organization starts up, someone must provide some money to get it going. For a church, this is likely to be in the form of donations, or possibly a loan. For a commercial business, this is known as capital. The difference is that capital means that the provider of money owns the business in some way, such as by being a shareholder, partner or proprietor. For a church newly founded by £1 million in donations, the first double entry is:

- Debit bank £1 million; credit donations £1 million.

As the accounts have debits and credits posted to them, the balances will go up and down, and sometimes change from being a debit figure to a credit figure. Depending on what the account is, a debit balance represents:

- an asset
- an expense
- the reduction of a liability or
- a trading loss.

Conversely, a credit balance represents:

- a liability
- income
- the reduction in value of an asset or
- a trading profit.

If every transaction from the first one has debits and credits of the same amounts, the total of all debit balances must always equal the total of all credit balances. In traditional book-keeping, the bookkeeper starts preparation for the year-end accounts by producing a list of all debit and credit balances (after some year-end transactions have been entered). This is known as the **trial balance**. In commercial accounts, these figures are then allocated to either the balance sheet or the profit and loss account to produce the financial accounts.

One final convention worth noting is that numbers in **brackets** around a figure represent a debit where you expect a credit, or a credit where you expect a debit. For example, if a list of amounts owed to suppliers includes the figure (£127.34), that means that instead of us owing the supplier £127.34 he owes us £127.34. This could arise if the supplier agreed to take back goods after we had paid for them, or if we overpaid him or paid him twice, or he agreed a retrospective discount. In adding up a column of figures, numbers in brackets are subtracted.

Books

Recording every single transaction in a journal can be tedious. In practice, it is more convenient to use **day books** and **cash books**. These, with the journal, are known as **books of prime entry**. Each book deals with a particular area of accounts, such as petty cash, purchases or payroll.

A day book simply lists all entries of a similar type, such as all donations received, or all bills paid. Periodically, usually once a month, these transactions are totalled, and expressed as a single transaction. For a purchases day book, the transaction will have one credit figure for the account 'purchases' and may have a dozen or more separate debits for each type of purchase.

There should be one cash book for every bank account, even with the same bank. There should also be a cash book for every petty cash box.

If you have a credit card on the church's account (which is un-likely), each credit card is also a separate account. Note that a *debit* card is not a separate card, as a debit card is simply a means to make a payment on a bank account.

The payroll has its own day book. The monthly transaction from the payroll is in the form:

Debit: employer's national insurance
              gross pay
              statutory sick pay and other statutory pay.
Credit: PAYE income tax
              national insurance (employer's plus employees')
              net pay.

All these monthly totals from each book of prime account are expressed as a double entry whose elements are debited and cred-ited in the **nominal ledger**. This is the master accounting record into which all transactions are ultimately recorded, and from which the trial balance was taken.

When Queen Victoria reigned, these books were exactly that – bound volumes in which all the numbers were dutifully writ-ten, often in beautiful copperplate handwriting. The book-keeper was, not surprisingly, the keeper of these books. Such books are still readily available from stationers, but most accounting is now done by computer, where each 'book' is simply a separate com-puter account.

Although the form has changed, the underlying principles have not. The 'book' may be a computer file, and you may not be aware of what is being debited and credited, but all the above is exactly what your software is doing for you.

Incidentally, bookkeeping, bookkeeper and bookkeepers are the only words in English with three consecutive double letters. There is no reason whatsoever why you need to know this, other than it provides momentary relief from a tediously boring sub-ject. Because this fact is so irrelevant, it may be all you remember from this chapter.

Ledgers

Double-entry book-keeping gives totals for accounts but pro-vides no breakdown. For example, figures for 'Creditors' and 'Debtors' tell you how much you owe and are owed but do not say to whom or by whom. For that, separate records are kept outside the double-entry system, known as **memorandum accounts**. All ledgers, other than the nominal ledger, are memorandum accounts outside the double-entry system. The purchase ledger or bought ledger records your creditors to whom you owe money; the sales ledger records your debtors who owe you money.

When using a computer system, this procedure is also invisible. At data entry you are asked to enter the name of the payee or payer, and this is automatically posted to an account in that person's name, in addition to being posted to the double-entry account.

Valuation

All accounting transactions are entered at the figures when the item was bought, sold or the transaction otherwise occurred. However, items change their value. Over time, cars become worth much less and houses become worth much more. The value of all the stationery you bought is worth less simply because you use it, so there is less of it. All these factors are dealt with by accounts in different ways.

The loss of value of a fixed asset is dealt with by **depreciation**. This only appears in accounts prepared under the accruals basis; depreciation does not appear in income and expenditure accounts. At its simplest, you decide how long an item is likely to last and divide the cost by the number of years. Suppose you decide that an electronic organ costing £6,000 will last fifteen years (which is probably about right). You 'write down' the value of the organ by £400 a year so that it is worth nothing after fifteen years. The journal entry each year is: debit depreciation (an expense) £400; credit fixed asset £400. So after one year, the organ is said to be worth £5,600; after two years £5,200 and so on. Financial Reporting Standard FRS 15 generally limits depreciation periods to a maximum twenty years.

Depreciation is in effect the 'cost' of an asset wearing. Note that it is not a fund to buy a replacement organ after fifteen years, which may cost much more than £6,000 in fifteen years' time. If you want to build up funds to replace an asset, that must be a separate fund in your accounts.

Depreciation is not likely to be a significant factor in any church accounts, as a fixed asset is written off over its 'useful economic life' where economic life is measured in terms of how long something will help you earn a profit. When your activities are not run for a profit, this concept becomes meaningless. However, churches can be required to depreciate fixed assets over their estimated useful life.

Some assets, particularly land and buildings, increase in value; this is known as **appreciation**. Where a balance sheet is prepared, appreciation is reflected by regular valuations. FRS 15 requires a full valuation every five years, with an interim valuation three years after a full valuation.

Concepts

The accountancy profession has developed various concepts, conventions, bases, policies, principles and other basic rules which are assumed to have been followed unless stated otherwise. These basic rules have been known by various names.

Financial Reporting Standard FRS 18 gives five **accounting principles**:

- going concern
- accruals
- consistency
- prudence
- separate valuation of assets and liabilities.

Going concern

This means that the organization will continue for the foreseeable future; it is not about to go bust. The opposite is **forced realization** where the entity expects to cease its activities, which usually means that its assets, particularly fixed assets, will be worth much less. This principle applies to churches and voluntary bodies as much as to commercial bodies.

Accruals

Revenues and costs are matched to the same period. This means that you do not put the income from an activity in one year and the costs in another. This concept only applies when not producing a receipts and payments account, as explained on page 73.

In a receipts and payments account, you record the income and expenditure when received, regardless of the period to which it relates.

Consistency

What you do one year, you do the next. However you decide to classify income or expenditure in one period is followed in all future periods. Sometimes, changed circumstances or experience may lead you to change your policy. That is fine, provided the change is noted in the accounts.

Prudence

You do not anticipate income but do anticipate expenditure. This concept is sometimes referred to as 'assume the worst'. In most cases, prudence is only relevant for accruals accounting.

Separate valuation of assets and liabilities

This policy was only introduced as such in 2000, unlike the others which were formally adopted in 1971 and were widely followed before then. It simply means that each asset and liability is valued separately and not netted off. If you owe XYZ £100 and XYZ owes you £500, you show a creditor of £100 and a debtor of £500, not a debtor of £400.

While these five are regarded as accounting policies, there are many other discernable fundamental concepts, of which two deserve particular mention.

Substance over form

This means that you look at the financial reality rather than the legal form. For example, if you lease a photocopier for several years, you do not own the photocopier. The lender (known as the lessor) or the lender's finance company legally owns the photocopier and you (the lessee) simply pay a regular fee to use it. However, the financial reality is that the photocopier is one of your assets in that you have the use of it to help your work on the same basis as if you did own it. So that is how it is shown in your accounts.

Materiality

This means that you do not bother with trifles. Accounts are meant to paint a picture, and you need not worry about amounts which are so small that they are not noticed in the picture. You still keep accounting records accurate to the nearest penny. So if the bank credits your account with 2p interest one month, you debit that 2p to your account in the name of the bank to ensure that the bank statement reconciles. However, you do not show 24p as a source of income in the annual accounts; you lump it in with other odd bits of income as 'Investment income' or 'Other income'.

There is no fixed percentage below which an item becomes immaterial, though 5% is mentioned in a few specific instances. Materiality is a subjective consideration based on size, nature and circumstances.

The concept of materiality is one which church treasurers often have difficulty in understanding or accepting. It is perhaps best explained in that the accounts are a picture where the artist wishes to draw attention to the subject. So you should not include detail which draws attention away from the subject. Your painting should be by Renoir rather than Constable.

Historic cost convention

In practice, all accounts are prepared under the **historic cost convention**. This ignores the fact that money loses its value through inflation (explained on page 67).

When inflation is around 2%, this does not matter much. When inflation is 20%, £5 at the beginning of the year is the equivalent of £6 at the end. Two methods of **inflation accounting** were developed to deal with this, known as current purchase power and current cost accounting. They were set out in Statement of Standard Accounting Practices SSAP 7 and 16 respectively. Neither commanded much support and both were repealed. SSAP 7 was repealed before it even took effect. Since SSAP 16 was repealed in 1985, there has only been one abandoned attempt and some guidance notes on inflation accounting.

It is normal for accounts prepared on the accruals basis to state that they have been prepared under the historic cost convention, even though there is no real alternative.

There is a separate international standard (IRS 29) for accounting in **hyperinflationary economies** where inflation exceeds 100% over three years. Such inflation rates still occur in some African and South American states. Typically, such high inflation is accompanied by social disorder and collapse of government. Basically it requires the accounts to be restated in a stable currency.

Contingencies

A contingency is an asset or liability the value of which cannot yet be fully determined.

An example is a contested insurance claim or a legal action. The existence of the asset or liability may be known with certainty but the amount which the church may receive or have to pay is not known at the time the accounts are drawn up.

The prudence concept is that a contingent liability is shown in the accounts at the highest figure which the church may have to pay, while a contingent asset is not shown in the accounts at all. In both cases, the contingency must be explained in notes to the accounts.

Liquidity

Liquidity is the ease with which an asset can be turned into cash. Cash is therefore the most liquid of assets. Assets in order of decreasing liquidity are:

- cash
- prepayments of future liabilities
- debts owed to you
- certain investments
- stock for sale
- other investments
- fixed assets.

Accounting standards

In 1875, Mr Justice Quain was hearing a bankruptcy case at the Bristol Assizes in which he deplored the loss of bankruptcy business 'from gentlemen solicitors to an ignorant set of men called accountants – one of the greatest abuses ever introduced into law'. Similar sentiments were expressed nearly a century later in 1971 when Rolls-Royce went bust despite accounts saying it was worth a fortune because of all its investment in the RB211 aeroplane engine.

Although the Institute of Chartered Accountants in England and Wales issued Recommendations on Accounting Principles from 1942, accounts were still largely subjective, with accountants free to classify and present figures how they wished. The collapse of Rolls-Royce forced the pace to have some tougher rules.

In 1970 and 1971 the various accounting bodies formed what became known as the Accounting Standards Committee (ASC) which prepared standards that the accounting bodies issued. They were known as Statements of Standard Accounting Practice (SSAPs) of which twenty-five were issued. They were brief documents outlawing some practices, specifying others, and sometimes requiring additional information to be provided in notes. Compliance was enforced by the accounting body disciplining any member who departed from an SSAP without good reason. There is no known instance of any accountant being so disciplined.

On 1 August 1990 the ASC was replaced by the more powerful Accounting Standards Board (ASB) which issued standards in its own name. At the same time it became a legal duty on companies and certain other bodies to follow accounting standards. The new standards are known as Financial Reporting Standard (FRSs) of which twenty-seven had been issued by the end of 2004. Several FRSs had been amended. Previous SSAPs remained in force, though they are gradually being replaced by FRSs.

There is also an Urgent Issues Tax Force (UITF) which issues abstracts dealing with specific accounting problems, such as how to account for the cost of setting up a website. There is a separate Auditing Practices Board (APB) which issues Statements of Auditing Standard (SASs) and other documents. Many of these statements are preceded by exposure drafts (EDs), financial reporting exposure drafts (FREDs – really!) and discussion documents. In

comparison with SSAPs these tend to be long and theoretical documents which can read like theological dissertations.

UK standards comprise SSAPs, FRSs, UITF abstracts; plus
SORPs, international accounting standards, other ASB guidelines, and the various Auditing Practices Board standards and
guidelines.

From 1 January 2005, European law insists that companies
listed on a stock exchange must comply with International Accounting Standards (IASs) issued from 1973. From 2003, the
IAS issues International Financial Reporting Standards (IFRSs)
instead. In general, UK accounting standards have been issued
or amended to comply with IASs and IFRSs. Although unlisted
companies, and bodies other than companies, such as churches,
do not have to comply with IASs, the ASB has decided that in
general they should.

In addition to issuing its own statements, the Accounting
Standards Board recognizes other bodies which may issue statements known as Statements of Recommended Practice (SORPs).
There was a suggestion that they be called Statements of Accounting Practice until it was realized that this abbreviated to SOAP
and allusions of laundering. SORPs are produced for thirteen different sectors, including charities. The ASB does not endorse or
frank SORPs but produces a negative assurance statement that
the SORP is not inconsistent with other accounting standards.

The Charity Commission issues the SORP for charities. Much
of this book is based on the contents of this SORP. Although a
SORP is *recommended* practice, and therefore is not mandatory,
a church or charity which departs from a SORP without good
reason could find itself in difficulty.

SORPs have gained some legal authority under Financial Reporting Standard FRS 18 on accounting standards which require
a relevant body to:

- follow accounting policies generally consistent with the relevant SORP
- state which SORP is relevant
- state how far the accounts have been prepared in accordance
  with the SORP
- explain any departures from the SORP, giving reasons for the
  departure and quantifying the changes if the SORP had been
  followed.

'True and fair'

In the UK, company accounts must be 'true and fair'. This expression is currently contained in Companies Act 1985 s.393 although it was first introduced in 1947 to replace the previous 'true and correct' requirement.

Church accounts prepared under the accruals concept (i.e. those with a turnover above £250,000) must comply with the 'true and fair' concept.

It is worth considering these two requirements of truth and fairness, and particularly to note that accruals accounts do not have to be 'correct'. Indeed they cannot be correct, because the accruals concept introduces subjectivity and opinion into the accounts. An opinion cannot be 'correct' in the sense of being the only right answer, but an opinion can be reasonable, in the sense of being within a range of acceptable answers. This is not so for a receipts and payment account which simply records the *facts* of what money has been received and paid during the year.

Accruals accounts are said to be like a picture. Different artists produce different pictures but they can be recognized as being of the same subject.

Truth simply means that something is what it appears to be. A picture of a bowl of flowers should show a bowl of flowers and not something else that looks like a bowl of flowers. Similarly, accounts should represent what has really happened in the entity during the period. The figures must be produced from proper accounting records, even though it may be possible to produce more than one set of figures.

Fairness means that the picture gives a proper overall view of the finances. It is possible for a picture to be true but not fair, such as a photograph from such an unusual angle that it is not obvious what the item's true shape is. Suppose a preacher says, 'There are those who say that God is dead, but I believe God is alive.' For a person to report that the preacher said 'God is dead' is true in that the preacher did say those words, but it is hardly a fair representation of what he said.

This concept is important in accounting because it is the king of all concepts, reigning supreme over all other laws, accounting standards, concepts and conventions. If an accounting standard does not give a true and fair view, you do not follow the standard. You give the true and fair view, and note where you have departed from the standard and why.

Accountancy profession

The accountancy profession is not united in the way that doctors and solicitors belong to a single body. Neither are the various bodies federated in a structure as engineers are. There are six accounting bodies which have a royal charter, namely:

- Association of Chartered Certified Accountants (ACCA)
- Chartered Institute of Management Accountants (CIMA)
- Chartered Institute of Public Finance and Accountancy (CIPFA)
- Institute of Chartered Accountants in England and Wales (ICAEW)
- Institute of Chartered Accountants of Ireland (ICAI)
- Institute of Chartered Accountants of Scotland (ICAS).

These six bodies also make up the Consultative Committee of Accountancy Bodies (CCAB).

Members of ACCA are called chartered certified accountants, of CIMA chartered management accountants, and members of the last three bodies are called chartered accountants. These terms are all misleading as the accountants themselves are not chartered; it is the body to which they belong that is chartered.

Various attempts have been made to integrate these bodies, but there has been no successful merger between accounting bodies since 1957.

CIMA specializes in management accounting and CIPFA specializes in public sector accounting, including charities. All six bodies have equivalent standing, with differences being historical or geographical rather than in standard. The last three bodies have a policy of representing 'chartered accountants' as the only properly qualified accountants, which view is not supported by law.

Members of the accounting bodies have the following designatory letters after their name:

Body	Designatory letters
ACCA	ACCA or FCCA
CIMA	ACMA or FCMA

Body	Designatory letters
CIPFA	CPFA
ICAEW	ACA or FCA
ICAI	ACA or FCA
ICAS	CA.

Other UK accounting bodies are:

- Association of Accounting Technicians (AAT)
- Association of Authorised Public Accountants (AAPA)
- Association of International Accountants (AIA)
- Chartered Institute of Taxation (CIOT)
- Institute of Financial Accountants
- Institute of Internal Auditors (IIA)
- Society of Practitioners and Insolvency.

An auditor is a member of AAPA, ACCA, ICAEW, ICAI or ICAS who has the relevant practising certificate issued by that body. Since 1996 AAPA has been a subsidiary of ACCA; its members qualify through another body.

There is also a specialist body called the Association of Charity Independent Examiners, founded in 1999. Full members of this Association are allowed to conduct an independent examination (but not a full audit) of a church or charity. Full members have the designatory letters FCIE.

7

Annual Reports

Form

An annual report on the finances is required for all charities and companies, and also by the rules of almost all church organizations.

An account is where the management answers to the members; the management provides an account of what it has done with the members' money and on the members' behalf. The annual report is the means by which the church practises stewardship.

Although accounts are intended primarily for the benefit of church members, they have other uses. They may need to be submitted to other bodies such as the Charity Commission (unless the church has excepted status), and Companies House (for a charity which is also a company). Charities Act 2006 now requires all churches to submit accounts if they have annual income above £100,000, even if the church has excepted status. They may need to be produced to the tax authorities. The accounts will usually need to be submitted to a central church authority.

Churches in the UK known to have excepted status are:

- Baptist Church
- Church in Wales
- Church of England
- Congregationalist Church
- Independent Evangelical Churches
- Methodist Church
- Presbyterian Church
- Presbyterian Church in Wales
- Roman Catholic Church
- Society of Friends
- Unitarian Church

Scottish and Irish charities are currently not required to submit accounts to the Charity Commission, so the issue of excepted status does not arise.

It should also be remembered that churches with excepted status may be required to prepare accounts under the rules of the church denomination.

Even if there is no legal requirement to produce annual accounts, this may be regarded as good practice.

Basic points

The contents of the accounts are now largely governed by The Charities (Accounts and Reports) Regulations 2008, and by the Statement of Recommended Practice of 2005 issued by the Charities Commission (commonly known as the Charities SORP).

It must be stressed that all regulations simply prescribe the *minimum* amount of information that must be disclosed. A church is always free to make additional disclosures.

There are some basic points which must be understood about annual reports on the finances:

1. The annual report comprises both numbers and narrative

The annual report comprises more than just a set of accounts. There must be a written report also.

2. The annual report is of the council or trustees, not the treasurer

The annual report is that of the church council or trustees (or equivalent), even though it may be called the treasurer's report. This means that the council or trustees must first discuss and formally approve the report, including the accounts. See page 103.

3. The report must be published as a single document

The annual report on the finances must be published as a single document. It is not acceptable for part of the report to be published with other parts to follow. Whatever information is required to be published must be included. This is now a legal requirement under the Charities Accounts Regulations 2008 mentioned above.

It is permissible for the annual report on the finances to be included with other annual reports if the church so wishes. In the Church of England, the other statutory reports are:

- churchwardens' report
- report on the parochial church council
- report on the electoral roll
- report on deanery synod.

There is no legal obligation on the minister or anyone else to give any other report. They may do so if they wish, and such reports may be bound with the report on the finances.

4. *The report must be accompanied by any auditor's or examiner's report*

Where the accounts must be audited or examined, that report must accompany the annual report. The Church of England and many other denominations do not allow the church members to approve unaudited or incomplete accounts. Neither may the meeting allow the churchwardens or church council to approve the accounts.

If the accounts are incomplete or unaudited, the meeting must be adjourned until the accounts are complete and have the necessary audit or examination report. Even if there is no specific rule in your church requiring this, such a rule can be implied, as without it the whole point of producing accounts is defeated.

5. *The annual report must be published*

This means that the accounts must be reasonably available to members. This does not mean that every member has the right to be given a free copy on paper, though this is the ideal. It is permissible to display the accounts on a noticeboard.

6. *The accounts must either be wholly RPA or wholly accruals*

The accounts must be wholly prepared on either the receipts and payments account (RPA) basis or the accruals basis. A church may only use RPA if its turnover is below a set limit (see page 69). It is not acceptable for some of the accounts to be prepared under RPA and other parts under the accruals basis.

7. *The members must approve the accounts*

The members should be allowed a reasonable opportunity to see the accounts before the meeting where they are asked to approve them. Members should have the opportunity to ask questions and make comments on the accounts (see page 123). The members must formally vote on a motion to 'accept' the accounts. This does not mean that they necessarily agree with everything in the accounts. It does mean that they consider the accounts sufficiently true and fair to be acceptable.

Anything less than an overwhelming majority for such a motion is a matter of concern for the church. If the motion to accept the accounts is lost, the meeting must be adjourned until an acceptable set of accounts is prepared. In such an eventuality, the treasurer should seriously consider whether he still has the confidence of the church members.

8. *All accounts must be headed*

Every annual report must *on every page* state:

• the name of the church or other church body
• the type of account
• the accounting period or date to which it relates.

This is a point which is so obvious that it is often overlooked.

9. *Note how the date relates to the accounts*

Receipts and payments accounts, statements of financial activities, and profit and loss accounts all relate to a *period* of time, usually one year. Traditionally the period is dated according to when it ends, so these statements are described as 'for the year ended 31 December 2xxx'.

Statements of assets and liabilities, and balance sheets relate to a *moment* in time, usually the end of the accounting period. These statements are described as 'as at 31 December 2xxx'.

10. The accounts must be signed

The accounts must be formally approved by the council or trustees or equivalent and signed by someone on their behalf, usually the treasurer.

The treasurer must sign the accounts on the statement of assets and liabilities or the balance sheet. Strictly speaking, it is not necessary for the signature to appear on copies of the accounts made available to members, though this is good practice. It is essential that the accounts state that they have been signed, by whom and on what date. Similarly it is good practice for the audit report to bear the auditor's signature. The inclusion of a handwritten signature helps to personalize the accounts.

11. The annual report must not assume prior knowledge

Account descriptions and narratives must not assume that the reader is familiar with the workings and jargon of the church. You may understand such things but you are intelligent and knowledgeable, which is why you are the treasurer. The average church member has no idea of what is meant by an archdeacon, ciborium or diocesan quota. Also remember that church accounts are read by people outside the church.

Be particularly careful about using abbreviations. If you refer to a donation from the MU rather than Mothers' Union, someone will wonder why the Musicians' Union is supporting the church. The author of this book was once concerned by a General Synod report on clergy pay which kept referring to what is considered adequate by the CSA. This concern was only relieved when explained that this referred to the Central Stipends Authority and not the Child Support Agency.

12. The report must clearly identify the church or other body to which it relates, and to the period to which it relates.

There must be no doubt about what church or churches are covered by the report, or to what year or period it relates.

In the Church of England, the annual report is of "The Parochial Church Council of . . ." In other denominations, the report may be of the trustees or diaconate.

If the church is a registered charity, the report must state its registration number and principal place of business. The names of the trustees (or equivalent) must be listed unless there are more than 50 trustees. In such a case, the list may be restricted to 50 trustees.

Where a church is run by trustees, it is also necessary to state:

- how the trustees are constituted
- how trustees are appointed
- method of recruiting and appointing trustees
- details of any person or body entitled to nominate trustees.

Timetable

Producing the annual report is not something to be started the week before the annual meeting with church members: it must be planned and timetabled.

The start of the process is the **accounting date**. This is the day in the calendar year to which the accounts are made up. The Church of England and many other denominations stipulate that the accounts must be made up to 31 December. In other words, the **accounting period** is the same as the calendar year. This applies even if the church did not exist on the previous accounting date. While accounts are usually prepared for a year, they may be prepared for a shorter period in the year that the church starts or ceases and in some other circumstances.

You must know in advance if you are preparing RPA (receipts and payments accounts) or accruals accounts.

The Association of Church Accountants and Treasurers suggests a timetable on these lines:

5 January	Obtain all bank statements
31 January	Ensure all transactions are entered
31 January	*If preparing accruals accounts,* make accruals
7 February	Receive statements from any other account holders, such as hall hiring secretary, magazine editor, etc.
14 February	Close the books
28 February	Prepare the accounts
31 March	Receive auditor's or examiner's report
14 April	Publish the accounts
5 May	Annual church meeting
6 May	Send copy to church authorities.

These are typical dates of a typical sequence of events. The timetable may need to be adjusted to your own circumstances.

Many treasurers prefer to **close the books** sooner than six weeks after the year-end, but you should not close them sooner than two weeks as this does not allow sufficient time to receive final details. Closing the books means that you do not make any further entries in the accounts for that year. If something significant happens after you have closed the books, you disclose it by a note to the accounts.

Closing the books is of less importance for RPA accounts than for accruals accounts. Under RPA you simply record payments when received or paid. If you pay a telephone bill on 2 January 2012, that goes into the 2012 accounts regardless of the period to which the bill relates.

Under accruals accounts, you may need to consider income and expenditure that will not be known until after you have closed the books. Examples include telephone bills, water rates and tax refunds under Gift Aid. Here you accrue an estimate of what you believe the figure will be. Once you have estimated the figure, you do not adjust it when the bill or payment comes in and you know the exact figure. If the amount is significantly different, you may disclose that difference as a note to the accounts. What is important to remember is that when you close the books, they stay closed.

Another departure from the timetable above may be to insist that you receive accounts from any other fund-holders sooner, and prepare accruals only after you have received those accounts.

Having produced the accounts, they must be submitted to the church council, diaconate, trustees or equivalent body in whose name the accounts are put to the members. Ideally they should have the draft accounts at least one week before they meet. The treasurer should attend that meeting.

The council or equivalent must satisfy itself with the integrity of the accounts. Ideally this should be a unanimous decision, though a majority decision is acceptable for a council. A council member or other trustee who does not accept the accounts should attempt to resolve the disagreement, first with the fellow members, and then with the auditor or examiner. If that does not resolve the matter, the dissenting member should raise the concern first with the central church authorities and then with the Charity

Commission. It should be remembered that the members are not asked to *agree* the accounts as if they were treasurer; members are asked to *accept* the accounts as a reasonable presentation of the church's finances.

Receipts and Payments Accounts

The receipts and payments account (RPA) basis is only permissible for a church with an annual turnover below £250,000 in England and Wales, below £100,000 in Scotland, or of any size in Northern Ireland. The use of RPA is *permissible*, not mandatory, so such a church may decide to use the same accruals basis required for larger churches. Before 1997, churches prepared an income and expenditure account which was similar to an RPA.

Independent churches and charities which are incorporated as limited companies must use the accruals basis regardless of size. It is also possible for the trust deed of an independent church to specify that the accounts must be prepared on the accruals basis, or in accordance with accounting standards, or to give a true and fair view. All those expressions mean that accruals accounting must be used. A church which is seeking grants may be required to provide accounts on the accruals basis and could find it difficult to obtain a grant using RPA accounts.

Finally, it is a fundamental concept of accounting that accounts are consistent from year to year. If a future year's accounts are likely to be prepared on the accruals basis, it may be desirable to adopt the accruals basis as soon as possible. Although it is permissible for a church to move from the accruals basis to RPA, such as if its income declines significantly, this is generally not recommended.

RPA accounts comprise:

- a receipts and payments account;
- statement of assets and liabilities; and
- notes to the accounts.

Note these terms. It is a receipts and payments account, not income and expenditure, nor profit and loss. The term 'Income and expenditure account' implies that the accruals basis has been used. Similarly the statement of assets and liabilities must not be called a balance sheet.

The receipts and payments account simply states how much has been received and spent under various categories. There are no strict rules on what categories must be used. The treasurer should err on the side of keeping the categories few, so as to present an account which paints a clear picture. Include all receipts and payments according to when received or made. A cheque received or paid at the end of the year may not be cleared by the bank until the next year. It is still included in the year of receipt or payment.

If the church has different funds, a receipts and payments account is prepared for each fund. Receipts and payments which are not part of any other fund are classed as **general fund**.

Receipts are apportioned according to the purpose of the receipt, not how it is made. It is irrelevant to the members how much was paid by cash, cheque or standing order. You may wish to analyse receipts and payments under sub-headings according to their purpose.

Typical 'Purpose' sub-headings would be:

Income	**Expenditure**
Voluntary giving	Related to the work of the church
Events and activities	Grants and charitable giving
Income from trading	Support costs
Income from investments	Publicity
	Church administration

Payments should similarly be under a few headings, though here it is likely that you will want to provide more analysis. This is done by notes to the accounts.

The figures for each sub-heading are totalled under a single line. A total is indicated by a double underline under the figures. (On Microsoft Word this is achieved by first typing control + shift + D. You repeat this to end the double underline.) A single underline below a total (i.e. a figure that appears between two single lines) is a sub-total which is added to other sub-totals. A double underline means that the figure is a total and not added to the numbers listed below.

Some treasurers do not like the idea of using single lines to indicate sub-totals and prefer to create a second column for the current year so that the sub-total is set to the right of the amounts. If that method is used, there should still only be a single column for the comparative figure for the previous year.

The figures for the current year are given nearest to the descriptions to which they relate. In the next column you give **comparative figures** for the previous year. An item must be included if there was a figure for either the current or previous year. If there is a nil balance for both years, the item may be excluded. If there is a nil balance for one year, that is better indicated as an amount of o rather than a dash, which could be misunderstood.

At the bottom of the receipts and payments account, you give a figure for the surplus, if the receipts exceed payments, or deficit, if the payments exceed receipts.

The receipts and payments account ends by adding the surplus or subtracting the deficit from the balance of funds brought forward from the previous year, to give the new balance of funds carried forward to the next year. The 'brought forward' figure for the current year must be the same as the 'carried forward' figure from the previous year.

It can be useful to use **bold type** to draw the eye to the key figures on the page, such as the total of receipts and of payments for the year, and to the surplus or deficit. A deficit is indicated by putting brackets round the figure.

An example of a receipts and payments account is shown in Figure 5. This example indicates probably the maximum amount of detail you should publish. It is permissible simply to print the sub-total figures without the detail.

Figure 5. St Gertrude's Church, Lower Snoddington
Receipts and payments account for year ended 31 December 2011

GENERAL FUND	£	2010 £
Receipts		
Voluntary giving		
Pledged giving [or stewardship]	58,263	56,104
Collections [or loose collections]	2,210	2,340
Other donations	0	2,000
Income tax recovered	22,103	21,089
	82,576	81,533
Events and activities		
Magazine sales and advertisements	1,506	1,420
Christmas fete	4,220	4,516
	5,726	5,936
Income from trading		
Hall lettings	8,479	8,266
Income from investments		
Interest on deposit account	1,004	989
Total receipts	97,785	96,724

Payments

Related to the work of the church

Diocesan quota [or similar payment]	42,109	40,083
Church expenses (see note 2)	9,110	8,724
Minister's expenses (see note 3)	1,206	1,243
Church hall running costs (see note 4)	8,130	33,099
	60,555	83,149

Grants

Missionary giving (see note 5)	7,102	6,995

Church administration

Church office (see note 6)	14,260	16,887

Total payments	81,917	107,031

Surplus (deficit) for the year	15,868	(10,307)
Cash and bank deposits brought forward 1 January	45,102	55,409
carried forward 31 December	60,970	45,102

CHURCH ROOF FUND

Interest on deposit account	401	387
brought forward 1 January	9,810	9,423
carried forward 31 December	10,211	9,810

When preparing accounts, the treasurer should note points on which questions may be asked (see page 123). In these accounts, the two significant points are:

- the church has moved from a deficit to a surplus
- the reason is because of a large reduction in church hall expenses.

The treasurer should know why.

In this example it can be seen that the income is very close to the £100,000 limit for RPA accounts. The treasurer should switch to accruals accounts for the next year.

Statement of assets and liabilities

A church which prepares a receipts and payments account should also prepare a statement of assets and liabilities. This must not be called a balance sheet as it is not one, even though it is similar. For the same reason, the figure on the statement should not be referred to as the church's net worth or accumulated reserves or any such statement, which is also incorrect.

The **assets** of the church may include:

- cash and bank deposits
- other monetary assets (such as loans made by the church, interest due, tax refunds due, insurance claims submitted but not yet paid, sums owed to the church for magazines or hall lettings)
- investment assets
- fixed assets owned by the church

and that is the order in which they should be listed.

The first three categories are relatively straightforward to value in most cases. The figure for cash and bank deposits must be the same as the carried forward figure for the current year in the receipts and payments account. Where funds are of different types, such as restricted and unrestricted, they must be shown separately.

Fixed assets can present a problem in terms of valuing. How do you value a nineteenth-century church building, its original cost, the cost of rebuilding it, the cost of building a new church of a modern design, the value that the site could be sold on the open market? These are likely to give widely different figures, none of which would mean much.

Because of this the SORP (Statement of Recommended Practice) says that heritage assets (see page 118) may be excluded from the statement completely. However, all assets not valued on the face of the accounts should be mentioned in the notes to the accounts. Where assets are listed, the amount for which the asset is insured is usually acceptable.

Guidance from the Church of England's Business Committee of General Synod says that any asset which has been **consecrated** is excluded from the accounts. In the Church of England, consecration is a legal process which formally restricts land and buildings to sacred use. Furnishings, ornaments and vessels may also be consecrated, though the procedure for disposing of them is less onerous. This restriction does not apply to items which have been **blessed** or **dedicated** as this does not change their legal status. These general principles apply to churches of all denominations, though it should be realized that words like 'consecration' and 'blessing' can have different meanings.

The **liabilities** of the church may include:

- amounts owed for utilities, such as electricity and telephone;
- PAYE and other outstanding deductions for staff at year-end;
- collections made but not forwarded at the year-end; and
- balances on any loans or borrowings by the church.

If a church has not paid its full diocesan quota or other payment due to a centralized church body, but intends to do so, the unpaid balance is a liability. An unpaid liability should usually only be excluded if the central church authority has excused payment.

If a liability relates to an asset, such as a loan against a building, that fact must be mentioned in the notes to the accounts.

Liabilities may be added together, particularly when the amounts are small. In many cases, a church may have zero liabilities.

The statement of assets and liabilities has sub-totals but no totals and may look like Figure 6.

**Figure 6: St Gertrude's Church, Lower Snoddington –
statement of assets and liabilities as at 31 December 2011**

		2010
	£	£
Monetary assets		
Current account	1,468	1,201
Deposit account	8,743	8,609
	10,211	9,810
Debtors: hall fees outstanding		
(see note 7)	450	0
	10,661	9,810
Fixed assets (at insurance value)		
Church hall	100,000	100,000
Other assets	20,000	20,000
	120,000	120,000
Liabilities:		
bills and expenses outstanding		
at year-end	1,002	816

Contingent liability:
the church has agreed to donate £600-worth of Christian
   books to the college due to open in the parish within
   the next two years.

Approved by the parochial church council on 15 March 2012
and signed on its behalf by J. Bloggs, treasurer.

Notes to the accounts (RPA basis)

A set of accounts is completed by the narrative report. This provides such further information as is necessary to aid the understanding of the accounts. It must be remembered that the notes
to the accounts are part of the accounts which the council or
trustees must have approved and which the members are asked
to approve.

The notes are numbered from 1. Traditionally, note 1 refers to the basis under which the accounts have been prepared.

Notes 2 onwards cross-reference to figures on the receipts and payments account, and the statement of assets and liabilities. These notes may themselves be a mixture of accounts and text, giving a further breakdown of the figure in the accounts and a description of to what the figure relates.

Further notes may identify contingent assets (see page 91), arrangements to create or wind up specific funds, and any change in church policy which affects the church accounts.

An example of notes to the accounts is given in Figure 7.

Accruals basis

Any church of any size may use the accruals basis, and a church above a certain size must use the accruals basis (see page 69).

Under the accruals basis, the church must produce:

- a statement of financial activities (SOFA);
- a balance sheet; and
- notes to the accounts.

Statement of Financial Activities (SOFA)

The statement of Financial activities is abbreviated to SOFA, so we will take as read all the jokes about padding and being comfortable. The main points to note about a SOFA are as follows.

1. Funds must be distinguished

The SOFA must show separate figures for each type of fund (e.g. restricted, designated, etc.). This is usually done by putting each fund type in a separate column.

2. Comparative figures must be shown

Figures for the previous year are shown as an additional column. It is not necessary to distinguish fund types for previous years.

3. There must be no netting off

Sources of income and expenditure must be shown at their full value. There may be several activities which generate both income and expenditure, such as bookstall, magazine, refreshments, fetes and hall lettings. It is not acceptable for the SOFA to show only a 'profit' or net income figure.

4. *Items must be included when 'recognized'*

Income is recognized when it is:

- certain in amount;
- legally enforceable; and
- either received or likely to be received.

In practice, most income is recognized when it is received. Income recognition may be an issue in such areas as negotiating a sale of land or settling a legal dispute.

Expenditure is recognized when:

- some consideration (see page 153) has been received for it, or
- a legal or constructive liability to pay has been created.

So expenditure for something which has been ordered but not received is usually not included (though if this expenditure is significant it may be disclosed in the notes to the accounts). A constructive liability arises when a church has resolved to pay the money, such as a donation to a mission or charity.

The SOFA is constructed in accordance with the format shown in Figure 8.

This format may look formidable, but is fairly straightforward when you get used to it. Not every figure may exist: many churches will have no figures for F and G, for example. That means it can omit the rows for F, G and H. It is likely that only the unrestricted funds will have entries in all the rows. The other funds are likely to have little movement.

Incoming resources are:

- collections, donations, legacies, tax recovered under Gift Aid and the like
- significant donations in kind (such as piano or photocopier) at cost or value
- gross income from fund-raising activities
- operating activities in the course of the church's mission, such as sale of magazines, and charges for attending a course

**Figure 7: St Gertrude's Church, Lower Snoddington –
notes to the accounts for the year ended 31 December 2011**

(Note 1) The accounts have been prepared on the receipts and payments basis.

The general fund is for the furtherance of the normal purposes of the church and is not subject to any restrictions on its use.

The church roof fund is a restricted fund which may only be used for the purpose of maintaining or replacing the church roof.

The church building has not been included in the statement of assets and liabilities as it is a heritage asset which could not easily be sold. Church fittings, vessels, ornaments and art are excluded for the same reason.

(Note 2) Church expenses comprise:

	£	2010 £
Heat, light, water and other utilities	2,068	1,977
Insurance	1,100	1,100
Repairs and maintenance	3,033	2,468
Music expenses	1,240	1,240
Candles and other altar requisites	601	596
Other expenses	1,068	1,343
	9,110	8,724

(Note 3) The minister is employed by the central church authorities. The parish pays for his travelling expenses, telephone and other incidental costs.

(Note 4) The church hall running costs are:

	£	2010 £
Heat, light, water and other utilities	1,305	1,288
Insurance	340	330
Repairs and renewals	6,485	31,481
	8,130	33,099

Extensive rebuilding work was undertaken in 2010 and completed in 2011.

(Note 5) The church's donations comprise:

	£	2010 £
Christian Charity in England	3,102	2,995
Christian Charity in Asia	2,000	2,000
Christian Charity in Africa	2,000	2,000
	7,102	6,995

The church has revised its policy of giving, and will now be donating 10% of all voluntary giving in the previous year.

(Note 6) Church administration costs are:

	£	2010 £
Maintaining a church office	12,105	11,877
Stationery and sundry	2,155	5,010
	14,260	16,887

(Note 7) These fees have now been paid.
The church is also owed hire fees of £200 from Whizzo Promotions which is now in receivership.

Figure 8: Format of statement of financial activities

Description	Unrestricted funds	Designated funds	Restricted fund	Endowment funds	Total this year	Total last year
Incoming resources Total	A	A	A	A	A	A
Outgoing resources Total	B	B	B	B	B	B
Net incoming resources	A−B=C	A−B=C	A−B=C	A−B=C	A−B=C	A−B=C
Transfers between funds	D	D	D	D	D	D
Net incoming resources before revaluation and investment asset disposals	C+D=E	C+D=E	C+D=E	C+D=E	C+D=E	C+D=E
Gains and losses on revaluation of fixed assets for church use	F	F	F	F		F
Gains and losses on revalue or disposal of investment assets	G	G	G	G	G	G
Net movement in funds	E+F+G=H	E+F+G=H	E+F+G=H	E+F+G=H	E+F+G=H	E+F+G=H
Total funds brought forward	I	I	I	I	I	I
Total funds carried forward	H+I=J	H+I=J	H+I=J	H+I=J	H+I=J	H+I=J

- investment income
- proceeds on disposing of a church asset.

It is not necessary for every category of income to be put in the SOFA. Items of income should be aggregated as will aid understanding. If necessary, further analysis can be provided in a note to the accounts.

Outgoing resources are analysed in one of two ways, depending on whether total expenditure exceeds £250,000. If outgoing resources do exceed £250,000, they must be analysed between cost of generating funds and charitable expenditure.

Cost of generating funds includes such items as the cost of a stewardship campaign and the costs of fund-raising activities.

Charitable expenditure must be further analysed between donations to other bodies, costs in furthering the church's activities, and costs of management and administration. If the support costs for the first two items are significant (which is unlikely in practice) they must be shown separately.

As with all accounts, additional information may be voluntarily disclosed in the SOFA or notes to the accounts.

If the expenditure does not exceed £250,000, this basic analysis is not compulsory, but it remains advisable.

Balance sheet

A balance sheet is a list of the assets and liabilities of an entity at a moment in time: it is a financial snapshot. Churches with a turnover above £250,000 must produce a balance sheet.

However, a church balance sheet has some significant differences from a business's balance sheet. In particular, a charity balance sheet does not say how much the charity is worth. Its function is stated in the SORP to provide 'information about the liquidity of assets and general solvency'.

A church's balance sheet must show these items:

- fixed assets
- movable church furnishings
- investments
- current assets
- liabilities.

In business, the term 'fixed assets' means anything which is owned by the business but is not consumed in the course of business. It thus includes buildings, machines, furniture and vehicles. It can even include intangible assets such as patent rights, copyrights and scientific know-how.

For churches, the definition of 'fixed assets' is much narrower. First of all, you exclude heritage assets completely. (Before March 2005, these were known as 'historic and inalienable assets'.)

Heritage assets are those items which cannot be disposed of without a faculty or similar permission from a central body. They are excluded from the balance sheet of any church or charity, provided they are:

- of historical, artistic or scientific importance;
- held to advance the preservation and conservation objectives of the charity; and
- acquired in a previous accounting period.

The commonest example is the church building itself.

Fixed assets other than heritage assets include buildings, furnishings, halls, contents, houses owned by the church, office equipment, vehicles owned by the church, and other property of the church, including significant items which have been donated.

Most fixed assets other than the value of land must be depreciated over their estimated life. Freehold property must therefore have its value apportioned between the building and the land, with only the building depreciated. Depreciation is explained on page 87.

It is normal to set a **depreciation threshold** below which assets are not depreciated at all but regarded as consumable items. The threshold depends on the size of the church's assets, but it is unlikely that you need set a threshold below £100. The idea of the threshold is that you do not have to depreciate staplers, ashtrays, coffee mugs, plastic trays and other small items. You only depreciate your larger fixed assets.

There are no set rules on the period or method for depreciating an asset. The commonest method of **depreciation** is simply to reduce the original cost by a proportion related to its expected life. So if you decide something has an estimated life of five years, you reduce its value by one-fifth each year. So a computer bought for £1,000 is valued at £800 after a year, £600 after two years, and nothing after five years. This is known as the **straight line**

method, because if you plotted values against time on a graph, it would produce a straight line.

The value of an item must never be more than its market value, which can be relevant for some items of electronic equipment where prices have fallen steeply. If the value of an item becomes worth less than its depreciated value, such as by being damaged, it must immediately be written down to that value.

Financial Reporting Standard FRS 15 gives considerable freedom in determining the period over which assets are written down. Its main requirements are that depreciation be charged over the asset's expected life, and assets are generally not written off over one year nor over more than twenty years. In practice, the following periods may be regarded as reasonable:

- motor vehicles: four years
- computer and electrical equipment: five years
- furniture and other items: ten years.

A walk round any church may show that it is full of furniture more than ten years old and equipment more than five years old. The fact that the church owns items which are regarded as now having nil value does not matter for the accounts. If this bothers you, you can always disclose these assets in a note to the accounts.

Land is subject to special provisions because it tends to increase in value. FRS 15 requires that land is not depreciated, and that both land and buildings are periodically revalued. They should generally be professionally revalued at least once every five years. You should make an interim revaluation (which you can do yourself) within three years of a professional valuation. The basis of the revaluation must be stated in the notes, including the professional qualification of the valuer.

Investments are all assets held to generate income or capital for the church. They should be included in the SOFA at market value on the balance sheet date. Any gains or losses made by disposing of investments must be disclosed in the notes to the accounts. Short-term investments may be included as a current asset rather than a fixed asset.

Current assets must be expressed at the lower of their cost and market value. This is unlikely to be relevant to churches. It would apply if you bought books at £5 to sell for £10, found they did not sell and therefore reduced the price to £2 to get rid of them.

You would have to reduce the value of stock from £5 a book to £2.

Debtors must be analysed between debtors and prepayments. A debtor is someone who owes you money. A prepayment is when you have paid money for something you have yet to receive.

Liabilities are sums which the church owes to other people known as **creditors**. The accounts must distinguish between current liabilities and long-term liabilities. A **current liability** is one which is payable within the next year. A **long-term liability** is payable more than one year after the balance sheet date. Long-term liabilities are rare in practice.

Provisions are contingent liabilities which should be included with current liabilities but be separately identified in the notes to the accounts. A provision is when the church sets aside money to pay for a liability which it knows it has, even though it may not be legally liable at the balance sheet date.

Notes to the accounts (accruals basis)

All the disclosures and further analysis which can be included in the notes to RPA accounts are also relevant to accounts prepared under the accruals basis (see page 73).

In addition the charities SORP requires the following specific disclosures. Many may not seem particularly relevant to churches, but you should remember that the SORP applies to all charities from Eton College to the Donkey Sanctuary, where such provisions may be more relevant.

The accounting basis must be stated, usually as note 1. Typically this will say that 'the accounts have been prepared in accordance with the Charities Act 1993 and the Charities SORP 2005 using the historic cost convention'. You may add any regulations which apply to your denomination. The historic cost convention is explained on page 90.

For **assets**, it is necessary to disclose the basis for the value shown in the accounts. This will usually be cost, valuation or revaluation. For fixed assets the basis of any depreciation charge (see page 87) and the depreciation threshold (see page 118) must be disclosed. You must also disclose the existence of heritage assets which have not been included in the balance sheet.

Incoming resources and **outgoing resources** should be accompanied by notes explaining the bases on which these items have been recognized. For outgoing resources (i.e. spending) it may also be necessary to explain how the expense has been allocated. If an expense has been apportioned between two categories of expenditure, the basis of that apportionment must be stated.

Grants and donations must generally be disclosed, analysed and explained unless they do not exceed £1,000 or 5% of total expenditure. In many cases, it is obvious what donations to the Missions to Seafarers and Royal School of Church Music are for. For bodies like Tear Fund and a local body with a name like the Snoddington Butterfly Appeal, a brief description of its purpose is appropriate.

Related party transactions must be disclosed. If a member of the church council is contractually engaged to do work for the church, that must be disclosed. This does not apply when a council member agrees to do some work for the church and is reimbursed his expenses. This provision allows church members to satisfy themselves that any such arrangement is proper.

Trustees' expenses must be disclosed. Trustees include church council members, members of a diaconate and any other member of a governing body, however described. If there are no such expenses, that fact must be disclosed. If there are expenses they must be aggregated and described. The names of the particular trustees should not be disclosed. The relevant note may say 'The church paid £123 (2011: £118) in travelling expenses and £120 (2011: £100) for child-minding to church members.' Such payments would be unusual in practice, but are possible.

If the church has insurance to indemnify the church for the trustees' fault or negligence, that must be disclosed, with details of the premium paid.

Total staff costs must be disclosed, split between gross wages and salaries, employer's national insurance, and pension contributions. The average number of employees must be stated in terms of full-time equivalents.

The number of employees who earn more than £50,000 a year must be shown in bands of £10,000. So you say how many employees earned between £50,000 and £59,999, how many earned between £60,000 and £69,999, and so on. If there are no employees earning that much, this fact must be stated.

If there are employees earning more than £50,000, details of any pension provision must also be disclosed.

Audit costs must be separately disclosed. If the auditor or examiner provides other services, such as basic book-keeping or financial advice, fees for those services must be separately disclosed.

Ex gratia payments must be disclosed. An ex gratia payment is one which the church is not legally obliged to pay but chooses to pay. Such payments need the express permission of the Charity Commission. The notes to the accounts must disclose the amount and nature of such a payment, and the date and authority for making it.

Material acquisitions need separate disclosure if they are so substantial that they reduce the liquid funds available for the church.

Presenting the report

It is normal for the treasurer to present the financial report at the annual meeting and answer questions. If the treasurer really cannot attend, someone else must be briefed to present the financial report.

The treasurer should not make a long speech nor give detailed explanations, however much the treasurer may enjoy his brief moment of glory. If you need to explain your accounts, you have not presented them well enough. The point of the presentation is to:

- draw people's attention to any significant points
- comment on any significant future implications
- say that you will answer any questions
- thank those who help you – those who count the collection, pay it in, type the accounts, and the auditor or examiner – and the members who contributed.

A typical treasurer's presentation will be similar to this:

> Thank you John. This year's accounts show that we made a small surplus thanks to some generous increases in pledged giving by a few members, and the welcome addition of new members to our stewardship programme. While we made a surplus and have a healthy balance, the church council has decided that we need to make extensive repairs to the church hall

which are estimated to cost £50,000 spread over two years. I am happy to answer any questions. In the meantime, I would like to thank those who count the collections each week, Fred my assistant treasurer for his invaluable help, particularly in banking the weeks' collections, Janet for producing these beautiful accounts from my scruffy handwriting, and Charles for again auditing the accounts so professionally. Finally, I would like to thank you all for your continued generosity in supporting the church.

Responses from church members can range from somnambulant obsequity as they approve the accounts without a murmur to a full-scale heated debate.

Answering questions need not be an ordeal. First, you should prepare for the occasion by:

- noting large differences between the current and previous years and knowing the reason;
- knowing instantly all decisions of the church council or equivalent that have financial implications; and
- having books or print-outs with you giving the breakdown of figures in the accounts.

If you do not know the answer, simply say that and offer to let the person know within the week. Don't apologize for not knowing. If someone really wants to know which tariff is used for the electricity bill, and whether another is cheaper, he should have given you notice of the question. You could reply that as the questioner knows so much about electricity tariffs, you will be pleased to give him copies of the bills so that he can answer the question for the church.

If you are aware of something in the accounts being an issue, prepare your facts.

Sometimes the treasurer can be a victim of the church's awkward squad whose questions are a symptom of an ongoing campaign, or whose questioner just enjoys being awkward or showing off his knowledge or has a pet hobby-horse.

The treasurer should not answer questions on policy such as why we gave only £100 to Christian Aid or why we spent £5,000 on a youth club for only five members. Your answer is because that is the church's policy. The minister, churchwarden or similar officer should be invited to answer the policy issue. Do not answer a policy question even if you know the answer or can think of a good reply.

The reply to a harangue is simply to say, 'I note your comments.' Never get cross, and never ignore a question. If someone is rude in putting their question, ignore the rudeness and just answer the question. Questions are more likely on payments than on receipts.

After a lively debate, the chairman can easily overlook the motion formally to adopt the accounts, which is what you have been debating. Hopefully, the chairman will not overlook thanking you for your hard work during the past year.

8

Insurance

Introduction

The responsibility for insurance rests with whoever in the church is responsible for looking after the fixed assets. In the Church of England this is the churchwardens.

Sometimes hard-pressed churches may seek to save money by not having full insurance cover. This is a fool's economy. Insurance is cheap the first time you use it.

Every day in Britain, ten churches suffer from theft, vandalism or arson, on average. Another way of looking at this is that, on average, a church can expect to suffer once every four years. The exact figure depends on the area, what security the church provides and how well the church is used.

What to insure

The basic rule is that you insure what you cannot afford to lose. You do not need to insure every hymn book and vase, because you can afford to replace them. This includes not only buildings and their contents, but other liabilities for which the church could be held responsible.

When you do need to insure, you should consider the amount of the **excess**. This is the amount of loss that you will bear. If the excess is £1,000 and you suffer a loss of £10,000, the insurers pay you £9,000 and you bear the loss of £1,000. An excess of £500 and £1,000 is usually affordable and can lead to a significant reduction in premiums as it avoids paying many small claims and restricts cover to large losses which happen infrequently.

If you have more than one set of premises, you should also be aware of **averaging clauses**. Suppose you have two churches, each insured for £1 million. You may be tempted to assume that it is most unlikely that both will burn down and so only insure them for a total of £1 million. If the policy has an averaging clause, the insurers will say that the churches were only insured for half their value, and so only pay you £500,000.

In any insurance contract, you insure:

- an asset
- against defined perils, for
- a maximum sum.

For this you pay a premium to the insurance company.

The **assets** you insure are those you would replace if lost. Heritage assets and other irreplaceable items may not need to be insured. If you lose an irreplaceable asset, what are you going to do with the money?

For buildings, your insurance should not be limited to the church building where you worship. You should also consider church halls, garden sheds, clergy houses and any church office.

The **perils** are stated in the policy, usually in the form of **exclusion clauses** which state what is *not* insured. You should check that you are insured for:

- fire
- theft
- malicious damage (such as vandalism)
- lightning
- explosion
- storms
- floods
- burst water pipes
- aircraft impact
- riot and civil disorder
- accidental damage
- terrorism.

For malicious damage, you should check whether that covers 'people who are lawfully on the premises'. If it does not, it means you are uninsured if someone walks into the church while open and damages your property.

Some of these perils are known as **acts of God**. These are as insurable as any other peril. The only perils for which insurance cannot usually be provided are war and nuclear explosions.

The **amount of insurance** cover required is usually more than the value of the insured item. For a building, the insurance must cover the removal of debris, temporary accommodation and professional fees, in addition to the rebuilding costs. For furniture and other items, the insurance should be for replacement cost, with no allowance for depreciation or wear and tear.

Other insurance risks

The church should consider insurance for things other than just buildings and contents.

Public liability insurance

This insures the church against a claim from an injured member of the public. This could be someone who slips on a wet floor, is hit by a loose slate or (incredibly) falls while trying to burgle you. Insurance cover should be for at least £5 million.

Employers' liability

This insures the church against claims by employees. This is a legal requirement; you can be prosecuted if you do not have this insurance. The church must display the certificate in a conspicuous place. Note that volunteers are not employees for this purpose.

Personal accident cover

This insures the claim for accidents incurred by volunteers engaged on church business. It should be appreciated that such a policy only pays out when the church is legally liable. The church may not be liable for accidents which are unforeseeable or are the fault of the injured person. The Compensation Act 2006 may further restrict the right to claim.

Money

In the form of ready cash, money can be insured against theft, loss or misappropriation. Insurance against misappropriation is called **fidelity insurance**.

Glass

This may need separate insurance cover from the building. If insuring stained glass, painted glass or engraved glass be careful exactly what you are insuring and the amount.

Consequential loss

This is that which is suffered by a loss of premises or equipment. It covers not just the loss of offering from non-attending church members but refunds of hire charges if the church hall becomes unavailable. You need to be clear what consequential loss the church may suffer.

Legal expenses

These can be insured in case anyone sues the church. Society has become litigious; it is possible to instruct lawyers on a contingent fee basis (where you only pay if you win); and there are companies aggressively marketing their services to secure compensation. Churches are not exempt from such claims. Legal expenses insurance is often surprisingly cheap and usually comes with a free telephone helpline.

Trustee insurance

This protects church council members and other trustees, however described, from any claim made against them personally. Such insurance cover must be specifically disclosed in the published accounts. As society becomes more litigious trustees are at personal risk. Such insurance only covers trustees while acting in good faith.

Building works

These usually need separate insurance. The JCT contract widely used (see page 157) specifies who needs to insure for what. In general, the church needs to arrange building works insurance for alterations, additions and repairs.

Travel insurance

This protects the church for losses of travel, such as cancellation, unreasonable delay, medical bills and the suchlike. This is usually arranged at the same time as the travel.

Vehicles

These must legally be insured for risks to third parties and to passengers: not to be so insured is a criminal offence under the Road Traffic Act 1988. There is no legal liability to insure the driver or the vehicle itself. You should ensure compliance with the conditions that are often attached to such policies, such as limiting cover to people over 25, or with three years' driving experience, or with a clean driving licence.

Choosing the insurance company

Your choice of insurance company should not just be based on the amount of premium charged. You should also consider:

- what 'excess' there is;
- the small print in the contract, particularly regarding your responsibilities; and
- the company's track record in meeting claims.

As with all suppliers, the best choice comes from recommendation. For an insurance company, this should be a church which has had to make claims.

The **small print** imposes duties on the insured. Read them and follow the details, as any non-compliance can make your insurance policy worthless. If the policy says the church entrance must have a five-lever deadlock and you have only a three-lever deadlock, the insurance company may refuse to pay a claim if you have a fire, even when the choice of lock would have made no difference. Not all insurance companies would be that unreasonable, but the law is on their side if they choose to be.

Your prime concern with an insurance company should not be whether its premiums are the cheapest, but how well it meets claims. A good benchmark is to consider Ecclesiastical Insurance, which was formed in 1887 by church members to provide insurance for the church. It is still owned by a charitable trust, while maintaining the highest standards of a UK-registered insurance company. It also offers considerable advice on security and related matters. Regard them as the benchmark, and see how any other insurer compares.

Security

It is not always considered necessary to lock a church during daylight hours. Indeed, Ecclesiastical Insurance generally recommends that churches are *not* locked during the day.

There are many obvious points for churches to follow:

- valuable items, such as chalices and crosses, should be kept in a safe when not in use. During the week, cheaper items should be used
- valuable items should be photographed, listed on an assets register, and possibly security marked
- electrical goods, such as computers and electric pianos, should be security marked and their serial numbers and other details recorded
- candles, matches, flammable material (such as piles of diocesan newspapers and service sheets) should be removed
- activities should be arranged so that the church has people in it when open
- keys should never be visible
- all access doors need the same level of security, including doors no longer in regular use
- independent professional advice should be taken before installing new alarms, locks or other security equipment
- outbuildings also need protection
- lighting acts as a deterrent
- have a safe.

Advice can be obtained from crime reduction officers in the Police, or from some insurance companies or independent consultants.

9

Fund Raising

Introduction

Fund raising is any activity the prime purpose of which is to raise funds for the church. A concert, outing, retreat or social activity should not be viewed as fund raising just because it made a surplus.

Churches have different attitudes to fund raising, ranging from those who see it as wrong when Christian stewardship is practised, to those who regard it as an integral part of church life. In general, a healthy church is one where stewardship funds all day-to-day expenses and mission work, while fund raising is kept for particular items of expense, such as paying for a new roof or hall.

It should also be appreciated that there is a considerable social and team-building dimension to many fund-raising activities. If a church does not conduct any fund raising, it should at least consider whether it is providing adequate social activities for pastoral purposes. If your stewardship is so good that you need no fund raising, consider having events and giving the proceeds to named charities rather than not having the social events.

Excellent advice on fund raising is contained in *The UK Church Fundraising Handbook* by Maggie Durran (SCM-Canterbury Press, 2003).

Setting up

Fund raising for a specific project should be undertaken by a sub-committee set up for the purpose. Its chairman should be someone dynamic. The treasurer should be a member of the sub-committee, but not its chairman.

There are specialist fund raisers. You should be careful about engaging one. They will often expect to be paid, regardless of how little you raise. If their fees are high, this can be counter-productive to donors. You should first look to find expertise more inexpensively. Perhaps a local church has recently conducted successful fund raising. Their mastermind will probably be only too delighted to attend your committee meetings to tell you how he achieved it. If you do need to engage the services of a professional fund raiser, consider inviting them to occasional meetings, rather than paying them a fee for overseeing the whole project.

The treasurer must know how much has been raised at every stage, and how much has been spent. For significant sums, it may be necessary to open a separate bank account.

The vision

It is important that you are honest in stating your aims when seeking funds. If you fail in your objective, such as not raising enough to build a hall, you could be liable to repay the funds.

The church must be behind your proposals for fundraising. It is easy for a keen individual to enthuse a church council but not the congregation. For any project, it is essential to have the support of the general church. This does not mean that every dissenting voice must be silenced; sometimes questioning from within can be constructive (though it usually isn't). It does mean that the vast majority of the church must be supportive or at least sympathetic.

Produce a simple explanation and have an open meeting to discuss it. The explanation can follow the **SWOT** principle used in business, identifying Strengths, Weaknesses, Opportunities and Threats of the proposal. Do not over-spirtualize your plans so that someone feels sub-Christian in expressing a genuine concern.

Sources of funds

There are broadly three broad sources of funds:

- donations from those within the church;
- donations from those outside the church; and
- grants from particular bodies.

Funds from within the church can be effectively raised by a **gift**

day. Members of the church are asked to sign pledges of funds in addition to their normal giving. The received wisdom is that a wider appeal for fund raising should not start until the church has already raised 60% of the funds needed.

Donations from those outside the church are usually confined to such activities as fetes and bazaars. Factors that need to be considered are:

- food served must comply with health and safety standards
- a licence is needed to serve alcohol and may be needed if the event includes live music
- the event overall must comply with health and safety regulations
- playing recorded music generally requires a performing rights licence.

The first three are administered by the local authority, the fourth by the Performing Rights Society, though most regular venues will already have an annual PRS licence.

From 1 November 2005, licences for alcohol and live music are issued by the local authority, though a licence for live music is not needed for church fund-raising events. The church will apply for a licence known as a **temporary event notice** (TEN). The event must:

- not exceed ninety-six hours (four days) duration
- be limited to no more than 500 people present
- not start within twenty-four hours of a previous licensed event finishing.

There is a limit of twelve events or fifteen days' worth of TEN events for any one venue.

The person seeking a TEN must:

- be at least eighteen years old
- not hold more than five licensed events a year (fifty if the person holds a personal licence)
- not be associated with someone so as to circumvent the previous provision (such as getting your wife to apply for a TEN for a sixth event)
- apply at least ten days before the event (though the council may specify a longer period)
- notify the police.

Grants from outside bodies may be sought, though usually such bodies are not concerned with the spiritual side of the church. They may make donations to preserve a historic building or work of art, or to maintain an organ for music concerts. Before making an application to such a body, you should find out its objectives and prepare a statement showing how your objectives meet that plan.

House-to-house collections

If you wish to collect money from house to house, such as while carol singing, you must have a licence under the House to House Collections Act 1939. The scope of the act includes going to pubs and business premises. A licence may only be issued to collect money for a charitable purpose. Plans to amend this law were proposed back in 1992 but have yet to be enacted.

The licence is issued by a senior police officer. Not all police stations are fully aware of their responsibilities, so be prepared to allow time for them to find the right form.

The House to House Collections Regulations 1947 state that collectors must:

- be at least sixteen years old;
- wear a badge identifying the person as a collector; and
- carry a certificate signed by the collector and an officer of the charity.

If the house-to-house collection is to raise funds for the church, it would seem that the certificate should be signed by the minister as the charity officer.

Money must be placed in a sealed box which may only be opened by the promoter in the presence of a witness.

Public collections which do not involve going from house to house, such as carol singing with collecting boxes in one place, must comply with local authority regulations issued under the Police, Factories &c (Miscellaneous Provisions) Act 1916 and Local Government Act 1972 s29. Collectors must be at least twenty-five metres apart. Contact your town hall for advice. Selling goods on the street may be regarded as a house-to-house collection.

Sponsorship

Strictly speaking, sponsorship is not really fund raising at all, as *sponsorship is a commercial transaction*. It is a contract between the church and another party. The church provides a benefit to that party in return for the sponsor's cash.

The benefit for the church may appear to be small, but it can be enough. In many cases, the sponsorship is little more than appearing to be community-minded.

It would be unusual for a business to sponsor a church's worship. However, many other events can attract sponsorship. These include:

- a building project
- new equipment
- a concert
- a youth activity.

Lotteries and gaming

Every church must decide whether it accepts a lottery or other form of gaming as morally correct. If you do decide to run a lottery, you must comply with the law, particularly the Lotteries and Amusements Act 1976 as amended in 1993.

A lottery is a distribution of prizes by chance, with no skill exercised by the players. If the players exercise any skill, there is no lottery, though it may still be regulated by the Act.

The two main types of lottery which a church may encounter are small lotteries and society lotteries. A **small lottery** covers tombolas, raffles and similar. No licence or procedure need be followed, provided:

- the lottery is not the main purpose of the event but is incidental to it
- tickets are sold at the event and cannot be bought before
- proceeds are devoted to a purpose other than private gain
- the cost of prizes does not exceed £250
- there are no cash prizes.

From 1 November 2005, it is put beyond doubt that alcoholic drink offered among prizes does not constitute a sale of alcohol requiring a licence.

A **society lottery** is a lottery that does not meet the conditions above, such as when cash prizes are offered or tickets are sold outside an event. Authorization comes from the local authority, provided:

- the ticket sales do not exceed £20,000
- ticket sales with any other society lotteries run by the church that year do not exceed £250,000.

A local authority may specify other conditions which must be followed. If these limits are exceeded, the church must register with the Gaming Board.

Gaming is a game of chance played for winnings. It includes bingo and whist drives. No licence is required if:

- the total payment made by each player does not exceed £4; and
- the total value of prizes does not exceed £400.

Above this limit, a licence is required from the local authority or Gaming Board.

10

Payroll

Introduction

The modern church may have many people who do paid work. In addition to the ministers, the church may engage a secretary, caretaker, cleaner, gardener, handyman, hall lettings secretary, youth worker, organist, accountant, and others.

It is essential that you identify who is legally regarded as employed by you, and ensure that you operate either:

- a full payroll system with tax deducted at source under the Pay As You Earn (PAYE) scheme, or
- use the Local Religious Centre exemption.

The church is committing a serious offence if it pays people without operating PAYE when it should. It could be liable to pay back tax and penalties.

PAYE is not just restricted to employees, but includes many other types of worker such as office holders. Church ministers usually are not legally employees, but they are still taxed as if they were employees.

You should note that PAYE also applies to benefits other than money. Such items as use of cars, medical insurance, training courses, accommodation and trips away can be taxable. There are very detailed rules about whether they are taxable and how the taxable amount is calculated.

There are several other matters which must be considered when employing staff, such as:

- national minimum wage;
- employment and trade union rights;
- maternity, sickness and similar rights;
- pensions;

- health and safety;
- human resources management.

There is a special construction industry scheme which may apply for building workers.

Some comments about income tax

Income tax is payable on wages, self-employed income, trading profits, pensions, investment income, and social security benefits that replace income (such as statutory sick pay). Income tax is also payable on certain benefits that arise from employment, such as a company car or health insurance.

Income tax is payable for a tax year which runs from 6 April to the following 5 April. (There is a long story behind these odd dates that involves Pope Gregory XIII and the Annunciation to the Virgin Mary.)

A book such as this cannot explain all the complexities of income tax. In outline, every person of any age is usually entitled to one personal allowance.

The personal allowance is:

- £7,475 for the year from 6 April 2011 to 5 April 2012
- £8,105 from 6 April 2012 to 5 April 2013, but this figure could change.

For future years, details of this allowance can be found from many sources, including the author's own website www.robertleach.co.uk.

Income tax is then charged at 20% on the next slice of income. Once someone has income from all sources of around £40,000, the tax rate increases to 40%. On income above £150,000 there is an additional rate of 50%.

Who runs the payroll?

When you accepted the job of treasurer, you should have established whether it is your function to run the payroll. It probably is, unless the church has specifically appointed someone else for the task. Even then, you will probably have to provide information for the purpose.

If the church has just a few people who are regularly paid, it is probably possible to run a manual payroll using the forms and tables provided free by HMRC. If either the church employs many people, or there are many complications in the payroll, it may be advisable to buy special payroll software or to use a payroll bureau.

Whoever runs the payroll must know what they are doing. Payroll is a specialist area, for which there is now a professional body giving qualifications separate from accountancy qualifications. Until the 1980s, payroll involved little more than looking up figures in tax and NI tables, making two deductions from gross pay, giving the employee net pay, making out a monthly cheque of tax and NI to HMRC and filling in an annual return. It is far, far more complicated than that now. Payroll is full of provisions which are rarely encountered, but which you must know if you do encounter them.

In addition, the whole PAYE and national minimum wage systems are now supported by a computerised system of fixed penalties which are automatically imposed for even minor breaches. A delay in submitting a tax return attracts an automatic penalty of £100, and can lead to a further penalty of up to £300 plus £60 for each day's lateness. Putting tax at risk can attract a penalty of £3,000.

It is only fair to say that considerable efforts have been made by HMRC to provide assistance to help employers comply. However all this does require considerable study by whoever runs the payroll.

Payroll is no longer a junior job like looking after the petty cash. It is too complicated and too heavily enforced with penalties. In practice, you must either study payroll yourself and buy software to run it, or use a bureau or accountancy firm to prepare your payroll. However you remain responsible if a bureau or firm makes a mistake.

Local religious centre (LRC)

One of the best kept secrets of the tax system is the Local Religious Centre exemption for churches. Even tax offices have not heard of it!

If *every one* of the people you employ earns less than the personal allowance for the year, you do not have to register for

PAYE at all. Instead you simply send the tax office a list of the names and addresses of everyone the church employed, and say how much they earned.

Details of the Local Religious Centre arrangements are found in the HMRC Inspectors' Manual at reference PAYE 23030.

As this is so poorly understood, this section is reproduced in entirety below. Remember this text is written for tax inspectors, not for taxpayers.

PAYE23030 – Employer records: employer types: local religious centres (LRCS)

A special arrangement has been agreed with 'The Churches Main Committee' so that a local religious centre (LRC), for example a parish church, can report payments made if they do not operate a PAYE scheme. An LRC guide to PAYE 2010–11 (Word 38KB) for the current year has been produced and can be printed locally when you receive an enquiry from an LRC.

Examples of such payments may include

• Payments to casuals
• Fees

If a PAYE scheme exists, the reporting system for payments is unchanged.

When Customer Operations Employer Section, East Kilbride receive information from an LRC, they will

• Trace the employer or individual
• Attach a memo with instructions and forward it to the responsible processing office
• If a new PAYE scheme is required, ask the processing office to set one up
  Or
• If an employer record is not found, and the information submitted suggests one is not required, they will scrap the papers after three years

If an employer record is identified by East Kilbride, on receipt of their memo you must

• Reply to any enquiry raised by the employer

And

- Remind the employer that as they already have a PAYE scheme the LRC Guide is not applicable

If a taxpayer record is in existence

- Casual income **must** be covered by allowances
- A PAYE scheme should not be opened at the LRC sub-source in respect of sums below the NIC lower limit

Any points of difficulty that can not be dealt with should be acknowledged then referred to PSN PAYE Technical, Shipley.

So who is included in payroll?

This is really two questions in one.

First the church must distinguish between volunteers and paid workers. Volunteers may be paid expenses, but no more. Paid workers must be paid the national minimum wage. It is possible for one person to be both a paid worker and a volunteer in different roles. However at all times there must never be any doubt as to whether a person is working for the church as a volunteer or paid worker. There can be no fudges or grey areas; it is one or the other.

Second, it must distinguish between the employed and self-employed. For an employed person, you must operate the PAYE system. For a self-employed person, you will usually require evidence that they are genuinely in business on their own account, and will need an invoice for each job. Note that a person is not self-employed just because you and they agree they are. If a person should be regarded as employed but you pay them as self-employed, you could be liable to pay the income tax and national insurance you should have deducted under the PAYE system.

Both of these distinctions can be difficult to make, so further details are given below.

In addition to this, there are some special tax provisions which must be considered when engaging people to do building work for you.

Worker or volunteer?

If someone works for the church and is not a volunteer, that person must be paid the **national minimum wage** (**NMW**). This was introduced on 1 April 1999. The rate is now revised every October.

The full rate applies to anyone aged 21 and over. There are reduced rates for workers under this age. The national minimum wage need not be paid for (among others):

- the genuinely self-employed;
- volunteers;
- certain apprentices and government-sponsored trainees;
- students on sandwich courses;
- au pairs and others who work within a family;
- work done under an informal arrangement (such as helping out);
- overseas workers;
- those working under a rehabilitation scheme;
- members of a religious community.

To be a volunteer, three conditions must be met:

- the body must be a church, charity, voluntary body or statutory body;
- the person must not be paid any more than reimbursement of actual expenses or a reasonable estimate of expenses; and
- the person receives no benefit in kind other than such accommodation and subsistence as may be reasonable in all the circumstances (which allows for 'house for duty' postings).

Note that for any job, a person is either a volunteer or a worker. There is no halfway house. It is illegal to agree to pay someone expenses plus £100 for 40 hours' work *even if the worker agrees*. If you engage a worker, you must pay the national minimum wage.

This does not apply if someone simply does some work when you have not engaged them. Suppose the organist decides to compose an anthem for a special occasion, or the parish secretary works a few extra hours to clear up some work. In neither case is the national minimum wage payable, as the church did not ask the person to work those hours.

Employed or self-employed?

There is no simple answer to this question. Some advice is given in a free HMRC leaflet number IR 56, which gives two lists of questions. If you can answer yes to most of one list, and no to most of the other, this can indicate whether someone is legally an employee. It is as imprecise as that.

You should consider everyone to whom the church pays regular amounts. It does not matter whether the amount is called a salary, wage, stipend, honorarium, fees or expenses. Nor does it matter whether the amount paid is the going rate for the job, or whether there is a written agreement. An informal arrangement for a nominal payment can be sufficient to bring a person within the scope of PAYE.

Employment tribunals are increasingly regarding church officers as employees.

In the same year, the Court of Appeal held that even a church **minister** could be an employee. The case was *New Testament Church of God v Stewart [2007] CA. The Times 20 November 2007*. The claim was brought by a minister whose pastorhood was terminated by the church council.

In 2011, Haley Moore succeeded in bringing a case (ref UKEAT/0219/10/DM) of unfair dismissal when sacked as a Methodist minister in Redruth, Cornwall.

In previous cases brought by an Anglican minister (1998) and a Methodist minister (1984), the tribunal had ruled that a minister could not be an employee because he was answerable to God.

In 2006, the House of Lords held in *Percy v Church of Scotland Board of National Mission* that spiritual duties did not prevent a Church of Scotland minister being considered as an employee. The Congregational Federation has advised its churches to regard ministers as employees for employment law.

In practice, only small house churches usually have their minister on the church payroll. Most of the main denominations run payrolls on a central or diocesan basis. However these rulings show that the tribunals and courts are increasingly regarding church workers as employees. In particular, the fact that someone's task has a spiritual or pastoral nature does not exclude them being an employee.

In 2007, Nottingham employment tribunal in a test case *A v B and C [2007]* held that an appointed church **organist** in the

Church of England is an employee of the incumbent and the church council. The duties of an organist under Canon B20 were held to be incompatible with being self-employed.

Be very reluctant to accept that anyone engaged by the church is not an employee.

Be reluctant to exclude anyone from the scope of PAYE and check with HMRC if you have any doubt. If the person disputes what HMRC says, that person must take it up with the tax office directly. If necessary, the matter can be settled by a hearing before Appeal Commissioners. The HMRC website has an employment status indicator (ESI) which may assist.

If HMRC accepts that a person is employed but accounts for tax under self-assessment, HMRC may issue an NT tax code which means tax is not deducted on the payroll. Otherwise, the church may either use the Local Religious Centre procedure as set out in the Inspector's Manual at section PAYE 23030, or include the person on a PAYE payroll.

It is probably advisable to consider everyone to whom the church pays any money on a regular basis and ask if there is any reason to *exclude* them.

Someone is *not* an employee if they are:

- only reimbursed for specific expenses with no personal profit;
- paid on a single occasion;
- clearly self-employed;
- employed by someone else; or
- where any payment is clearly a gift.

A Sunday School teacher does not become an employee simply because she is given £20 to buy some art materials, and returns with the items and gives back the change. However expenses are only outside the scope of PAYE if they are reimbursed at exact cost and no more. Any round-sum allowance must be taxed as earnings. Suppose you engage a groundsman for £100 a month to include materials. The whole £100 a month must be taxed. The groundsman may be able to claim the materials as expenses against his earnings, but that is a matter between him and HMRC.

Some expenses, particularly travelling, may be difficult to quantify. For these items, HMRC has agreed set rates which may be regarded as simply meeting the cost of travel without any profit. For travel by car, the rate (in 2011/12) is 45p a mile.

Someone paid on a single occasion is unlikely to be an employee. Examples include a visiting organist. However the regular organist may have to be taxed under PAYE.

Many people to whom the church pays money regularly may be obviously self-employed, such as the milkman and window-cleaner. Otherwise you should be reluctant to accept that someone is self-employed.

You similarly exclude a person whom you know is employed by someone else. In many churches, an obvious example is the minister, who is paid by a central body but receives expenses from the church. Do not attempt to put such a minister on your payroll.

A personal gift by way of testimony or thank-you does not count as taxable income, even if given as cash, such as a leaving present. Similarly a voluntary donation of cash to meet personal hardship, if unrelated to the person's work and in line with donations the church makes to others in similar circumstances, is not counted as taxable income.

Children who sing in the choir are specifically exempted from being regarded as employees by the Children and Young Persons Act 1933 s30(1). Children are entitled to the same personal allowance for income tax as adults, so it is unlikely that choir pay would be sufficient to become taxable anyway.

Registering for PAYE

The first step to setting up a payroll is to register with HMRC for PAYE. The easiest way to do this is on-line at the HMRC website at http://www.hmrc.gov.uk/paye/file-or-pay/fileonline/register.htm.

You are then given a User ID and must choose a password. This is sent by post. The process takes a week according to HMRC, though it is wise to allow longer.

The letter gives an activation code that creates a user file for the HMRC website. This must be entered within 28 days, or it expires and the registration process must be repeated.

Once registered for one tax, you are registered for all taxes except corporation tax which requires a separate registration. This can be useful if your church must account for VAT or income tax.

You should note that PAYE must now be operated on-line by computer. The old options of sending returns on paper have generally been repealed.

There was a facility for submitting paper returns if a person's religion prevented them using a computer. The only known groups to which the religious exemption applied were certain Brethren congregations and Orthodox Jews. This exemption is being withdrawn.

It should be appreciated that all PAYE filing is subject to strict deadlines, enforced by tough automatic penalties. Whoever operates the payroll must be properly trained in the use of the scheme. The HMRC website offers some training facilities. There are also commercially available training companies. The cost of a course may be less than the first penalty!

Many churches and charities run by volunteers have been caught by tax penalties. Although it is sometimes possible to appeal on ground of 'reasonable excuse', this can require the knowledge of a tax accountant which can cost more than the penalty.

To register, you must have to hand the following information:

- the name, address and proper name of your church. (Do you know its postcode for example?);
- when your first employee started or will start;
- how many employees you are likely to have;
- how frequently you intend to pay them (eg weekly, monthly etc);
- the official address for all communications (which may be the church office or your home address).

If you have registered for PAYE using paper returns, you must re-register on-line though you will only need to know your employer PAYE reference number and the Accounts Office reference. Both can be found on the yellow PAYE payment booklet.

HMRC will send you a starter pack including general guidance, with the forms and tables you are likely to need. HMRC also provides support teams who will, if you wish, visit you to help you set up the payroll and get yourself sorted out.

In recent years, HMRC has been the subject of much criticism by judges, Parliament, Chancellors and the accounting profession. Complaints relate to poor service, such as an inability to get matters resolved quickly by letter or telephone. The kindest comment the author can make is that HMRC acknowledges these issues and is putting measures in place to restore the service to a minimum standard.

When you are registered you are given a PAYE reference number in the form 123/A456 which must be quoted on all PAYE documents. You are also allocated a tax office which may now be hundreds of miles from where you work.

Payroll in outline

At its simplest, producing a payslip involves:

- calculating the person's gross pay;
- deducting income tax under PAYE;
- deducting national insurance; and
- paying the net pay to the person.

The tax and national insurance, plus employer's national insurance and (possibly) some other adjustments are paid to HMRC once a month or once a quarter.

At the end of the year, an annual return is completed which is sent to HMRC, and a summary for each employee is prepared of which one copy goes to HMRC and one copy to the employee.

It should be appreciated that payroll can become immensely complicated, but these steps can be looked at in a little more detail.

Gross pay

Gross pay is whatever the church and the individual have agreed between them. They can agree to a figure provided by someone else.

An employee does not have an automatic right to pay increases, even just to compensate for inflation. It would be unusual for pay rates to remain unchanged for several years without an increase, but this is a matter to be negotiated between the church and the individual. It is advisable to find a convenient month and review the pay rates each year from that month.

Deductions from pay

There are strict rules on what may be deducted from pay. An employer cannot make a deduction from pay just because the employee owes money to the employer.

The only deductions which may be made from pay are:

- income tax and national insurance;
- where a court orders deductions from earnings;
- where a local authority issues a council tax attachment of earnings order;
- certain payments for the maintenance of a child;
- where the employee has expressly authorised a deduction in writing;
- where the contract of employment specifically allows deductions;
- to correct a mistake on a previous payslip (not always allowable); and
- for certain stock or cash deficiencies in a retail operation.

Tax and **national insurance** are calculated by reference to a tax code and national insurance contribution letter, using either tables provided by HM Revenue and Customs or payroll software.

Employment law

Employment law is a vast complex discipline in its own right. This chapter can only highlight some of the main areas of consideration. Advice should be sought for further clarification on any of these points.

It is illegal to **discriminate** against someone because of their race, colour, ethnic origin, sex, marital status, pregnancy, disability or membership or non-membership of a trade union. In Northern Ireland, it is also illegal to discriminate on the basis of a person's political view. A woman must be paid the same rate as a man doing the same or similar work.

From 1 December 2003, it is illegal to discriminate against a person because of their **religion** unless that is a factor in the job. So a church is probably allowed to exclude a non-Christian from being a youth worker but would have more difficulty excluding for a post such as gardener.

Also from 1 December 2003, it is illegal to discriminate on grounds of **sexual orientation** (whether the person is homosexual) unless it is the church's declared and consistent policy not to employ such a person. This remains a largely untested area of law.

An employee must be given a written **contract of employment** within two months of starting work, unless the contract lasts for less than one month. An employee gains many employment rights after working for one year. Before engaging an employee, the employer must check that the person is allowed to work in the UK.

An employee must be given 5.6 weeks' paid **holiday.** For someone who works five days a week, that is 28 days a year. This includes public holidays. Note that there is no general entitlement to take a day's leave on a public holiday. This is a matter for negotiation between employer and employee. The eight public holidays include Good Friday and Christmas Day which may be the days when you particularly need the employee!

Note that the limit is 5.6 weeks or 28 days for the whole of the UK, including Northern Ireland which has ten public holidays. There is no additional leave when an extra public holiday is declared, such as for the Royal Wedding in 2011 and the Diamond Jubilee in 2012.

An employee cannot be compelled to work more than 48 hours a week.

Rules on **equal pay** mean that a woman must be paid the same rate as a man doing equivalent work. Also **part-timers** must be treated on the same basis as full-timers. All employees must be given an itemised **payslip** showing how their net pay has been calculated.

From 1 October 2004, an employee cannot be dismissed unless a **disciplinary procedure** has been followed. From 6 April 2009, the statutory disciplinary and grievance procedures have been replaced by less formal provisions based on the ACAS code of practice. If either the employer or employee fails to follow the proper procedure, any eventual settlement could be adjusted by up to 25% against the party at fault.

A dismissed employee may be able to claim for either unfair dismissal or unlawful dismissal or both. **Unfair dismissal** is where the reason for dismissal is unfair; **unlawful dismissal** is where the procedure for dismissal has not been followed. If an employer makes it impossible for an employee reasonably to continue working, the employee may be able to resign and claim **constructive dismissal.**

An employee must be given **notice** other than for a summary dismissal. The notice period is:

Length of service	Notice period
less than one month	none
1 month–2 years	one week
2 years–12 years	one week for each complete year
more than 12 years	12 weeks

Summary dismissal is when an employee's conduct is such that an employer cannot be expected to continue the employment, such as when the employee is guilty of theft or violence.

An employee who is made **redundant** may be eligible to claim redundancy pay, but care must be taken to ensure that the legal requirements for redundancy are followed.

Employees with sufficient working time may be eligible for **statutory maternity pay, statutory sick pay, statutory adoption pay** or **statutory paternity pay.** A woman who becomes pregnant while working for you acquires rights to maternity leave.

An employee is entitled to **paid time off** from work:

- for 5.6 weeks' holiday plus any extra entitlement in the contract of employment;
- to carry out duties as a trade union official, pension fund trustee or safety representative;
- for ante-natal care;
- for certain help for a disabled worker; and
- for study leave if under 18 and educationally disadvantaged.

An employee is entitled to **unpaid time off** from work:

- for jury service;
- for certain duties as a magistrate, councillor or member of certain statutory bodies;
- to look after dependants in certain circumstances.

It is stressed that employment law is a specialist branch of law where penalties and awards can be large. A church should ensure that any employment issue is dealt with properly by people experienced in that area. It is unlikely that a senior church officer, such as an archdeacon or diocesan secretary, will have the necessary skills.

Human resources

Human resources management (HRM) is the application of psychology to maximise the return from employees. Although this is more philosophical than financial, HRM is increasingly being linked to payroll.

HRM is an area where churches can easily get into the 'we've repealed the law of gravity' mindset. If a church was putting up a new building, it would not hold prayer meetings to find out how deep God wanted the foundations, nor how strong the supporting joists should be. The church would simply ask the architect or civil engineer, acknowledging that it makes little difference to the answer whether the building is to be used as a church or a warehouse.

Yet when we wish to build a church of people rather than stone, the received wisdom of HRM is too easily abandoned in favour of a religious-flavoured do-it-yourself philosophy. And we wonder why we see problems in the church.

HRM is a large subject, but we can briefly touch on a few basic assumptions. These principles apply mainly to paid workers of the church, though some can apply to volunteers also.

Maslow's hierarchy of needs identifies five levels of human need:

- self-actualisation;
- esteem;
- social;
- safety;
- physiological.

These needs should be met from the bottom up. A higher level cannot be satisfied until all lower levels are satisfied. Physiological means meeting the basic needs of food, clothing, warmth, shelter and health. Safety is the security that the job will last. Immediately we can begin to see why there are problems with poorly paid insecure ministers. Social needs include love and friendship. Esteem includes self-confidence, recognition and respect. Self-actualisation is when the person realises their potential for continuing self-development.

Volunteers are likely already to have the two lowest levels met, but still need to have needs from social upwards satisfied.

A distinction is made between **motivators** and **hygiene.** The former are those factors which encourage greater output. Hygiene are factors which do not themselves motivate but whose lack demotivates. Some examples are:

Motivators	Hygiene
achievement	pay
recognition	relationships
responsibility	quality of supervision
promotion prospects	working conditions
the work itself	fringe benefits

Note that pay is not a motivator. If someone believes they are being paid a fair rate for their work, further payment will not yield to greater productivity. However, someone who believes they are underpaid will be demotivated.

Demotivation translates itself in increased cost for the employer, such as by increased absence, increased staff turnover and reduced efficiency.

II

Contracts

Introduction

A treasurer is not normally responsible for overseeing contracts involving the church. However, the treasurer can become involved and so should have some knowledge.

At its simplest a contract is a legally enforceable agreement between two or more parties where each provides a benefit to the other. This benefit is known as a **consideration**. Usually you pay money to buy goods or services, but other contracts are possible.

Unauthorized purchases

A treasurer must not pay an invoice or expense claim unless he is reasonably satisfied that the expenditure has been:

- authorized by the appropriate church authority;
- provided as stated; and
- provided at the agreed price.

A church is legally either a corporation sole or a trust, either of which is as much a legal person in their own right as a human individual. However, such a legal person can only act through human agencies, who order goods and services. The separate branch of agency law only allows agents to act within their agreed authority, however.

If an agent acts within the authority given by the church, usually the church council, the church is legally bound to honour the contract. If the church authorizes a churchwarden to buy some gates, and the churchwarden buys poor gates, the church cannot renounce the contract. It may have a claim against the supplier if the goods are not of a satisfactory standard, but that is a separate issue. Authority can be implied, such as where someone has routinely ordered goods or services for the church which it has accepted on previous occasions.

If a person orders goods or services without authority, the church is not obliged to pay for them. In such a case, the supplier is legally obliged to minimize his loss, such as by taking the goods back. In some cases, this may not be easily possible, such as when the goods have been personalized for the customer (such as printed orders of service or embossed pew Bibles) or where the invoice is for a service already supplied. In such cases, the supplier may make a claim against the agent – whoever ordered the goods or services without authority. This applies even if the church did receive some benefit from the supply. A church must be able to control its funds through its own channels and not let anyone incur expenditure for whatever they wish.

The supplier may be told to claim against the individual who placed the order. This legal remedy is known as quasi-contract.

It is easy to see the strife that could follow from taking such a firm line with a maverick church member. In practice, the council may decide to reimburse all or some of the individual's costs. Factors likely to favour substantial or even full reimbursement include:

- how far the individual reasonably believed he had authority
- whether the church would have ordered the goods anyway
- what benefit the church has received.

Factors likely to favour little or no reimbusement include:

- that the individual has made unauthorized purchases before
- that the individual knew he had no authority
- the church does not want the goods or service
- the church received little benefit from them.

The decision of what to do must be made by the church council in full knowledge of the facts, and not by just automatically taking a soft or hard line. Such problems can be avoided by making clear to church officers exactly where their authority lies, and by telling major suppliers who is authorized to place orders.

Choosing a supplier

A church must be careful in choice of suppliers. A good practice is:

- ask other churches who they use and what their experience is
- do not assume that a member of the church is a good supplier
- always be reluctant to accept someone who approaches you
- do not put too much reliance on following up references provided by the supplier – a rogue may keep two or three customers sweet for that purpose.

A further test can be to consider how well it treats you *before* you are a customer. Ask yourself:

- When you call, do you get a person or a machine?
- Are letters answered promptly?
- Are your questions answered properly, or are bits glossed over?

A business which does not look after you when trying to get your business is unlikely to look after you once it has got it.

Read the contract

Remember that a contract is not binding unless you enter into it voluntarily. Read all the small print. If necessary, have someone experienced in business or legal matters to read it also.

Generally, all the terms must be settled *before* the contract is agreed. One party cannot impose new conditions on the other after the contract has been agreed. If you do not accept a condition, do not agree to it: ask for it to be varied or find someone else.

In some cases, it is not necessary for every last condition to be specifically agreed each time. For example, if you routinely engage an odd-job man at £10 an hour, it is reasonable to assume that you are agreeing that rate with him when you give him a new job. If you have agreed a detailed contract with a supplier, it is equally acceptable to agree a further contract on the same basis as the previous one.

If necessary, the courts can imply conditions into a contract where necessary to give it effect. If it is clear that the parties believed different things when they contracted, the courts may be able to void the contract. However, the courts will not amend or void a contract just because it is a bad bargain. If you have an opportunity to discuss the terms of a contract but choose not to do so, you are bound by that contract.

In some areas, particularly building work, there are standard contracts produced by bodies such as the Royal Institute of British Architects (RIBA). These are generally fair contracts, and may be accepted as such. However, you should still understand your responsibilities under the contract.

Engaging a contractor

Churches routinely engage the services of contractors to fix windows, floors, roofs, hedges, boilers, photocopiers, among many other areas. There should be no problem with this, provided certain basic procedures are followed.

In general, the larger the amount of money you are spending, the greater is the need for control. For small items, such as tuning the piano or pruning the hedge, it is probably sufficient to agree a price and for a church officer to tell the person to proceed without first obtaining quotations or references.

Some guidance on finding suitable suppliers and contractors is given later.

If you ask the price, ensure that you know whether you have an estimate or a quotation. An **estimate** is simply how much someone believes a job will cost. The supplier is not bound to supply you at that price. The supplier is simply giving you an indication of what he expects the cost to you will be. A **quotation** is a contractual offer which you accept to form a binding contract. Typically, a quotation has a time limit on it, usually a matter of weeks, before it expires. If you consider that an estimate is acceptable, you may ask for a quotation.

Assume that an indication of price is an estimate unless the document specificially states that it is a quotation.

Large building contracts

A church may have a major contract, such as building a hall or replacing the roof. Such a contract can easily exceed £1 million, far more than probably all other contracts for recent years put together.

Before starting on such a building work, you should ensure that you comply with relevant law regarding:

- planning permission
- listed building consent
- faculty jurisdiction, or other denomination-specific permission
- any covenants in force on the land
- obligations under Party Wall Act 1996
- obligations for archaeological sites.

Once the project has started, you must comply with Building Regulations and other laws and regulations.

The starting point for a building contract is the architect. Most churches have diocesan offices or similar central bodies which retain the services of a reliable architect, or at least have a list of recommended architects. The architect can:

- identify your requirements
- identify opportunities to meet those requirements, and constraints which may restrict them
- draw up plans
- provide advice
- set out procedures
- prepare a project brief
- prepare tender documents
- evaluate tenders
- advise on awarding the contract
- monitor the contract during construction
- inspect the finished work
- be available for any issues for a period after completion.

Most architects are members of the Royal Institute of British Architects (RIBA) which has standard contracts for projects. This includes a 'small works' contract for projects costing less than £150,000. Most building work in the UK operates under contracts issued by the Joint Contracts Tribunal (JCT) of which RIBA is a member.

The **JCT contract** asks the parties to state:

- the names and addresses of the customer and the contractor
- the description of the work to be done
- what statutory approvals the customer will obtain
- what facilities the contractor is permitted to use on site free of charge

- the price
- stage payments
- how long the work will last
- contractors' insurances
- what hours the contractor can carry out work
- whether the premises will be occupied during the contract period
- how disputes are handled.

The next step is for the church to appoint its own supervisor for the project. Ideally this is someone from the congregation, though this is not essential. The supervisor must be totally committed to this role, and not be someone who will 'try to fit it in' among other work. The supervisor must attend the site at least twice a week, and be prepared to walk round the site wearing welling-ton boots and a hard hat to inspect progress. The supervisor will carry a notebook, recording what the contractor says.

The supervisor must have necessary skills, preferably ones honed from dealing with builders before. The supervisor and builder must 'speak the same language'. Neither should be able to pull the wool over the other's eyes. If you have someone like that in your congregation, wonderful. If not, ask other local churches with whom you enjoy a good relationship. They may have some-one willing to do the task for you, perhaps for a reasonable do-nation to their church. If you cannot find such a person by that means, engage a consultant. This is an additional category of ex-pense, but such a person will almost certainly save you money in the long term.

The supervisor must meet regularly with the minister and churchwardens (or their equivalent), and attend church council meetings at appropriate intervals. The minister and senior church officers should occasionally accompany the supervisor when in-specting the site during construction.

The work on a major contract can be split into three catego-ries:

- fixed-price work
- contingent work
- time work.

Fixed-price work should be the bulk of the contract. The con-tractor is asked to quote a fixed price for the job, including all materials, labour and other expenses, and he does the work for that price. There should not be any 'extras' on a fixed-price contract. It has been known for a church to accept the lowest quote, and then find so many extras being added to the price that the work becomes the most expensive. A fixed-price contract must be exactly that – no variations because of anything unexpected, or because of illness, weather, supply problems and the like.

Even for a fixed-price contract, you must know exactly what is included. Unless otherwise allowed for, the fixed price should include:

- all plans and operating instructions
- fees for planning permission, listed building consent, etc.
- demolition of existing buildings
- removal of rubbish from the site
- fixed items such as kitchen units, sinks, boiler, safe, handrails, etc.
- paths, fences, gates, notice boards
- landscaping (e.g. trees, bushes, grass)
- VAT on materials
- site security
- site insurance
- storage of materials and equipment
- hire of equipment
- payments to subcontractors
- regular meetings with your supervisor.

Often a church will include some special items such as stained-glass windows, murals, sculptures, pipe organ, amplification and the like. The church will usually acquire these items under separate contracts. The main contract should specify how far the contractor is required to install these items or prepare the areas for their installation. There is no problem in the contract excluding any items listed above, provided that they are known and budgeted for at the start.

Old buildings often contain valuable items, such as plant, timbers, windows, doors and radiators. There should be clarity as to who derives the benefit from selling these items. A normal arrangement is for the church to identify the items which it wishes to sell itself, and for the builder to arrange disposal of the rest.

Although 'fixed price' seems the ideal, sometimes it is necessary to agree a price for **contingent work**. This arises when it is not easily possible to quantify a requirement, such as when it is not known how strong the roof beams are or whether an existing building contains asbestos.

A very common example relates to foundations. It is common for there to be no reliable records on what lies below the ground, though this can have a significant effect on the price for piling and foundations. The risk of such contingent work can be reduced by site testing, such as taking core samples in advance. This is a trade-off between incurring additional testing expenses against reducing contingent work. It is an area where the architect can advise you.

It is essential that contingency-triggering work is fully defined in advance, with the architect arbitrating in any dispute. For all contingent work, the supervisor is required to exercise a significantly greater degree of supervision.

Sometimes not even contingent work is sufficient to cover an eventuality. In such cases, it may be necessary to agree **time work**. This is paying by the hour, and should always be the last resort. This requires an even higher level of supervision, such as the supervisor remaining on site. Be very reluctant to agree any time work, and check timesheets exhaustively.

If you engage contractors for building work, you should check whether you need to deduct income tax under the **construction industry tax scheme**.

Tips before hiring tradesmen

The following tips have been prepared by trading standards officers.

- use tradesmen recommended by friends and family
- when making a booking, most tradesmen will give you a morning or afternoon appointment. If you are taking time off work, let them know just how important it is that they turn up – if they then fail to attend without good reason you should be in a better position to be able to claim some compensation
- look for a genuine address with a landline telephone number, rather than an accommodation address with a mobile number
- the biggest advertisements in a trade directory do not guarantee reliability; larger companies often employ sub-contractors who are paid on commission – the bigger the bill, the more they get paid

- make sure you agree a basis for charging before the work is started
- keep an eye on what they are doing.

How a supplier treats you before you are a customer is also indicative. If they treat you badly while trying to get your business, you are unlikely to be treated well when you *are* a customer. Indicators of a poor supplier are:

- telephone is answered by a machine asking you to press buttons
- calls left on an answering machine are not answered
- rudeness
- unwillingness to give straight answers to your questions, particularly on price
- missed appointments.

When the church is the supplier

Sometimes a church may be the supplier rather than the customer. A common example is when letting a hall.

There is no reason why a contract must be unfriendly to be legally binding. It is ironic that a church can have trained welcomers to create a friendly atmosphere, while the hall lettings contract does the opposite. A contract for the hire of a hall could start:

> We thank you for hiring our hall. We hope that you enjoy using it. To help us provide a service for you and other hirers, there are certain matters where we need your agreement. These are set out below. If you have any concerns about any of these matters, please speak to us before signing this agreement.

12

Property

Introduction

The law makes a distinction between owning and possessing property.

The **owner** has legal title; the **possessor** has actual custody. If you lend your property to someone, you remain the owner but the borrower is the possessor. The distinction can be vital, as many rights and duties are vested in the possessor.

Property is legally classified as either real property or personal property. **Real property** (or realty or real estate) comprises land in its various forms. **Personal property** (or personalty) comprises moveable items, such as goods and chattels. There are some significant legal differences. For example real property may only be bought by a written contract for which stamp duty land tax is payable.

Land may be possessed in several ways, particularly:

- freehold
- leasehold
- commonhold
- lease
- licence.

Freehold means that you own the land indefinitely, legally known as 'fee simple absolute in possession' under the Law of Property Act 1925.

Leasehold means that you hold the land until a predetermined date, which can be hundreds of years' time. Until that date you pay ground rent to the freeholder, which is often a nominal amount. After that date, the property reverts to the freeholder.

Commonhold is a creature of the Commonhold and Leasehold Reform Act 2002. The commonholder owns his own property and is automatically a member of a commonhold association which owns common parts such as corridors, stairs and access roads.

Lease is when property is let for a finite period, usually in return for rent.

Licence is when a person is allowed to use property without acquiring any legal rights, such as booking a hotel room.

In general, ownership of land means owning everything on the land, under the land and over the land, though there are many exceptions. A building is owned by owning the land it stands on.

Land law is a complicated subject in its own right for which professional help is often required.

Building work

Building work can require:

- planning permission
- listed building consent
- (in the Church of England) a faculty.

Planning permission and listed building consent are obtained from the local authority, who will usually advise you free of charge before you submit a planning application. A faculty is granted by the Chancellor of the diocese.

A church engaged in building work must:

- have proper plans drawn up
- know how the work will be funded
- supervise the building contract (see page 158).

Funding may require fundraising (see page 131). It will also need careful budgeting and monitoring. The budgets need to consider the running cost of the building once completed.

For repairs to the chancel of a Church of England parish church, there may be a **lay rector** who is legally obliged to maintain the chancel under the obscure Chancel Repairs Act 1932. Despite being a quirk of history, this right was upheld as recently as 2001 in the case *Wilmote Billesley Parish Church Council v Wallbank [2001]*. The lay rector argued that this breached his rights under the Human Rights Act 1998. He won the case but lost on appeal.

Be very careful about whether your work attracts VAT as this is a complex area where many churches have suffered problems. If the work does attract VAT, this adds 20% to your costs, which you cannot recover. In general, a completely new church building and certain building work to listed buildings are zero-rated. Other work may be standard-rated. You should also be aware of the listed places of worship scheme. This can allow some adaptations to a listed place of worship to qualify for a grant equal to the amount of VAT payable.

Stamp duty land tax is payable on the purchase of land.

Sale of property

The sale of land or buildings is more straightforward, though again consideration must be given to the tax consequences.

VAT can be a particular problem on the costs of sale. This may be avoidable by the church registering for VAT, and charging VAT on the sale which the purchaser may be able to recover. However, advice should be followed as there are other implications of adopting such a policy.

Churches are not liable for **capital gains tax** which is generally payable on property sales.

Sometimes land may be subject to a **covenant,** strictly a restrictive covenant, as there are other types. This can allow a landowner to impose restrictions on what may be done with the land. Before a sale is made, a check should be made for covenants as this can reduce the value of the land. Not all covenants are enforceable and those which are may be overcome, though this is a specialist area.

13

Legacies and Bequests

Introduction

In practice, a treasurer is not likely to need to know much about
the law on testacy. What happens in practice is that someone dies
and a solicitor writes to the vicar to say that an amount has been
left to the church, and arrangements are then made for payment.
A cheque is sent from the solicitor which the treasurer pays into
a bequests fund.

This section provides background information which may assist the treasurer if any queries arise.

Testacy

When someone dies the money passes under either the laws of:

- testacy, if the person left a will, or
- intestacy, if the person did not leave a will.

Whatever a person leaves on death is known as the person's
estate.

A person who makes a will is said to be the **testator**, and is said
to be **testate**. The estate is administered by an **executor**.

A person who does not make a will is said to be **intestate**. The
estate is administered by an **administrator**.

In these contexts, a female person is sometimes called a testa-
trix, executrix or administratrix. Their rights and duties are
exactly the same.

It cannot be stressed too strongly that all adults should have
a valid will. That is the only way to ensure that your wishes are
followed. If a married person dies with children alive, the surviv-
ing husband or wife does not inherit everything. Part of the estate
may pass to the children under the laws of intestacy.

Also, an executor has authority from the moment of death,

whereas an administrator only has power from when letters of administration are granted. There can also be a practical problem in that more than one person may apply for letters of administration, forcing the court to decide.

A person may make or amend a will at any time from the age of eighteen until the moment of death, provided the person has sufficient mental capacity. A will must be in writing, signed, and witnessed by two people who are not beneficiaries of the will. For a person of reduced mental capacity, it is advisable for one of the witnesses to be the testator's doctor, as the doctor could then testify to the testator's mental capacity should that be challenged.

It is advisable to review your will at least once every ten to twenty years to see that it still represents your wishes. It is also advisable to ensure that your family knows where they can find the will, and the name and address of your solicitor. It is helpful to document where your assets are (such as bank accounts, savings and investments). Sometimes these documents are kept with a draft of your funeral service.

An amendment to a will is usually called a **codicil**. This is executed in the same way as a will.

People should not put off making a will, as people can die at any age: death does not make an appointment.

A will may be revoked at any time from making it to the moment of death by:

- making a subsequent will or codicil which replaces the former
- destroying the previous will, or
- marriage.

Marriage automatically revokes a will unless the will identifies the person to be married and states that the will is to continue after marriage.

Divorce does not revoke a will, but removes the former husband and wife as a beneficiary or executor. Someone who wishes to include a former spouse must make a new will to that effect.

A will may be challenged on the grounds that the testator was subject to force, fear, fraud or undue influence. Also, a testator must make adequate provision for those dependent on the testator at the time of death, failing which the court may order adequate provision to be made, regardless of the terms of the will.

If it is known that a person made a will but it cannot be found after death, there is a presumption that the testator destroyed it.

This presumption may be rebutted by evidence to the contrary when it may be possible for a will to be admitted to probate having been reconstructed from evidence as to its contents.

Legacies

Words like 'legacies' and 'bequests' are often used interchangeably, though they have specific meanings.

A **legacy** is a gift of 'personal property' or personalty. This is anything except land. A person who receives a legacy is a **legatee**. This contrasts with a **devise** which is a gift of 'real property' or realty (or real estate) which is land, including buildings and anything else attached to the land. A person who receives a devise is called a **devisee**. A bequest is the gift of a legacy. A church may be a legatee or devisee.

There are four types of legacy:

- specific legacy
- general legacy
- pecuniary legacy
- residuary legacy.

A **specific legacy** is when a clearly identified item is left to a person, such as 'my car registration number . . .' The problem with a specific legacy is that if the testator no longer owned the item at death, the legacy fails by **ademption** and the legatee inherits nothing.

A **general legacy** is of identified property which is not distinguished from other property. An example is '500 shares in Sainsburys' without specifying which 500 shares. Some text books also identify a **demonstrative legacy** which is a general legacy identifying a fund, such as '£1,000 from my deposit account with Lloyds TSB'.

A **pecuniary legacy** is an amount of money. This may be stated in the will, e.g. '£10,000', or it may be calculated such as by reference to an index of inflation, or it may take the form of an annuity, payable in instalments.

A **residuary legacy** is whatever is left over after all other legacies have been paid.

A devise can be specific or residuary.

ᅠ

Failure of legacies

Legacies and devises may fail for many reasons, of which the commonest are:

- disclaimer
- ademption
- predeceasing
- divorce
- uncertainty
- being void.

Disclaimer is simply when a person says he does not want the item. No one can be forced to accept a legacy. The item then becomes part of the residuary legacy.

Ademption is when the item no longer exists. There are many rules on this, such as for shares in a company which has been taken over.

Predeceasing is when the beneficiary dies before the testator. This has now been amended by law so that a beneficiary must live for at least 28 days after the testator to inherit. A will may allow for predeceasing by saying that if the beneficiary predeceases the testator, the legacy passes to another beneficiary.

Divorce or separation means that legacies to the former husband, wife or civil partner fail, though the will otherwise remains valid. It is possible for a will to be phrased so that a former spouse inherits. It is also possible to make a new will to include a former spouse.

Uncertainty is where the identity of the legacy or beneficiary cannot be established with sufficient certainty. A legacy of 'a handsome gratuity' or to 'the son of X' (who had several sons) would fail.

Void legacies are those which contravene a law. This includes legacies against public policy, where a beneficiary witnesses the will, or where the legacy contravenes the law on accumulations and perpetuities.

Drafting a will

Drafting a will is a specialist skill which should be undertaken by a solicitor or similar person with those skills. Forms provided by stationers and charities should not be used.

A gift to 'my grandchildren' could mean grandchildren born when the will was made, who were born at the time of death, or including grandchildren born after the testator's death. 'Money' is another term capable of several meanings. The law will tell you what these terms mean, but it may not be what the testator intended.

Similarly a badly phrased clause can have unfortunate consequences. In the case *re Sinclair [1985]* the testator left a residuary legacy to his wife, or to a charity if she predeceased him. At death, he was divorced. The wife inherited nothing because she was divorced from him, and the charity inherited nothing because she had not predeceased him.

Inheritance tax

Inheritance tax is payable on estates above a threshold. However, no tax is payable on estate left to a church or other charity, or to a trust to be applied for the benefit of a church or charity.

Legacies to a church

A legacy to a church is valid provided it meets the other conditions for a valid legacy. Conditions attaching to a legacy may be a problem unless specifically clear. This is an area where professional advice is needed in drafting the will.

The first a church may know of a legacy is when a solicitor or executor contacts the church with the news. If the legacy has a condition attached, it will become part of restricted funds. If the condition is that only interest be spent, it will become part of the endowment funds (see page 11).

A legacy must not be included in the accounts until it has been received or until it is certain that it will be received. Other legacies notified but not received should be noted in the notes to the accounts.

If a legacy is without restriction to purpose, it is simply accounted for as a donation to the unrestricted funds.

Perpetuities

It should be noted that the law does not allow money or property to be tied up for ever. Under the legal principle of **perpetuities**, a disposition of property may only be vested for the lifetime of an individual (or the last living individual of a group) plus twenty-one years. Alternatively, a finite period of up to eighty years may be specified. For more recent estates, the perpetuities period may be 125 years.

14

Trusts

Introduction

A trust is an arrangement whereby one person holds property for the benefit of another. If you give a friend a pound to buy an ice cream for your son, you have created a simple trust. There are three parties:

- the **settlor**: you, who provided the property (the pound)
- the **trustee**: your friend, who has custody of your property
- the **beneficiary**: your son, who will get the benefit of the property.

It is possible for two of the three parties (but not all three) to be the same person. For example, you could have given your friend a pound to buy you an ice cream.

Trusts can be created as simply as that, though when land and property or large amounts are involved it is normal to have a written **trust deed** which sets out the rights of the beneficiary and the duties of the trustees. A trust can also be created by a will of someone who dies.

Trusts are more common than many people realize. For example, as two people cannot own the same piece of land in England, couples own property as a trust – a fact of which they are probably unaware. Trusts are also used for pension funds, inheritance tax planning, insolvencies and charities. It is the last of these with which we are concerned.

In addition to its own funds, a church may have some involvement with a separate fund held in trust.

Legalities of a trust

There are three legal requirements for a trust:

- certainty of intention
- certainty of subject matter
- certainty of objects.

In other words, there must be no doubt that the settlor intended to create a trust, what he contributed to the trust and for whose benefit the trust exists.

Types of trust

Trusts can be classified in various ways. In terms of legal form, there are four types of trust:

- statutory trust
- express trust
- implied trust (or resulting trust)
- constructive trust.

A **statutory trust** is one which is created by an Act of Parliament when an event occurs. For example, an executor dealing with the property of a person who has died is automatically a trustee of that property under section 33 of the Administration of Estates Act 1925.

An **express trust** is one which is deliberately created by the settlor. Most trusts dealt with by the church are express trusts.

A **resulting trust** is one implied by the conduct of the parties, such as when a person buys property for himself and another person.

A **constructive trust** is one created by a court. A common example is when the court renews a lease when the landlord has not.

Another classification is between simple trusts and special trusts. In a **simple trust** the trustees simply own the property until the beneficiary requires it to be transferred to him. A **special trust** is where the trustees have duties to perform.

Special trusts are further distinguished between ministerial trusts and discretionary trusts. A **ministerial trust** requires no more than ordinary business skills, such as in collecting rent and arranging repairs. A **discretionary trust** is where the trustees must exercise judgement. The beneficiary may be a class of beneficiaries, such as residents of a retirement home. The trustees may be required to consider who should receive payments or benefits, and of how much.

A final distinction is between private and public trusts. A **private trust** benefits one or a small group of defined people. A **public trust** benefits society in general, or a considerable part of society. Only a public trust may legally be charitable.

There are also special types of trust used in connection with inheritance tax.

Trusts found in churches

A trust may be held within a church other than by the church council, trustees or equivalent body. It is common for Church of England parishes to have funds held in a trust where the trustees are whoever is the incumbent and churchwardens. These funds are not part of the church's funds, though their existence should be noted in the annual report.

Some churches have **educational trusts** established under what is now the Education Act 1996 s.554. These include the so-called **three-fourteenths trusts** which arise when church school property is sold. Traditionally the incumbent had the use of the school building for Sunday and half of Saturday, which is the origin of the three-fourteenths rule. When a school closes, three-fourteenths of the proceeds remain with the parish in an educational trust administered by the incumbent and churchwardens. If the income exceeds £1,000 a year, the trust must be registered as a separate charity.

All **incumbent and churchwarden trusts** must either be registered as a separate charity or treated as a special fund of the church.

A **trust for ecclesiastical purposes** held by an incumbent and churchwardens, such as to maintain the church and churchyard, must have its funds held by the Diocesan Board of Finance as custodian trustee.

Where trust funds are administered by the church council, the trust funds must be included with church funds, usually as a restricted fund. Where the trust is administered by someone else, such as incumbent and churchwarden, the trust is regarded as a connected charity. Its funds are not included with the church funds but are noted. When a connected charity pays for items which would otherwise be the church's responsibility, that payment must be included in the church's income as a grant and the expenditure as church expenditure.

Sometimes all trusts need to be tidied up, particularly when the passing of years has made it less than obvious what the purpose of the trust was. Some methods for doing this are to:

- look for the original document which set up the trust. This may be a deed, constitution, Charity Commission scheme, will, resolution of a body, or a letter
- check whether a central registry or records office holds such documents (though do not expect their staff to do the searching for you)
- check with the Charity Commission to see if it has been registered as a separate charity
- if you believe the trust arose from a will, this may be traced from the Probate Registry.

Sometimes there can be problems when the trust deed (or equivalent) is found. A common problem is that the trust deed specified that the original trustees should appoint their successors but died without doing so. In such cases the Charity Commission can make an order appointing new trustees. The original objects of the trust may be outdated, obsolete or so similar to the objects of the church that to maintain a separate trust is pointless. The Charity Commission may allow the trust assets to be transferred to the church. A permanent endowment may have become so small that accounting for it is not worth the effort. The Charity Commission may allow you to spend the capital, ending the trust. The funds of the trust may have become small, when it is probably advisable to spend them all and end the trust.

Historically, many munificent trusts were established by benefactors for the relief of poverty. The welfare reforms of 1948 made many of these trusts redundant. Accordingly many **parochial trust** schemes were established which swept up these funds into a single body. Such trusts are outside the scope of the church, though the church is usually involved in their management. Many of these parochial trust funds are wealthy and can provide a useful source of assistance for needy people who do not qualify for any social security benefit.

Trusts for graves and private masses

Before considering charitable trusts, there is one halfway house that could be relevant for churches.

A general principle of trusts is that there must be a human beneficiary capable of enforcing it. For charitable trusts, the Attorney-General can enforce the trust on behalf of the public. If there is no beneficiary for a non-charitable trust, it cannot be enforced. George Bernard Shaw's will contained a provision to set up a trust to reform the English alphabet. This was not upheld, as an alphabet cannot bring legal proceedings to enforce a trust.

Against this strict rule, the courts have allowed what is known as a **trust of imperfect obligation** where there is no human beneficiary. The general rule is that the law will not stop a trustee administering such a trust but will not compel the trustee to do so. So if a lady leaves money in a will to look after her cat, the trustee may legally choose to do so, but cannot be compelled. This applies to sums left to erect or look after graves or monuments, or to say private masses for the departed. If a church accepts a sum for such purposes, it is morally obliged to do so, but is not legally obliged.

Note that a sum which is left to plant a tree is valid, as this benefits those who will see it. Also, a sum left for saying *public* masses is valid, as anyone may attend.

If there is no clear beneficiary, the trust fails. In the case *Morice v Bishop of Durham [1804]*, the court would not uphold a trust created in a will leaving a sum to the bishop 'for such objects of benevolence and liberality as [he] in his own discretion shall most approve of'. There was no clear beneficiary at all.

15

Tax

Introduction

In the UK, taxes are said to be either:

- direct; or
- indirect.

Direct taxes are taxes on income. National insurance is now generally regarded as a direct tax. Indirect taxes are taxes on spending. A full list of UK taxes is given below.

Taxes levied in the UK

Direct taxes	Indirect taxes
Income tax	Value added tax
Corporation tax	Customs duties
Capital gains tax	Stamp taxes
Inheritance tax	Excise duties
National insurance	Landfill tax
Windfall tax	Air passenger duty
Petroleum revenue duty	Insurance premium tax
	Climate change levy
	Aggregates levy

From 18 April 2005, all UK taxes are collected by HM Revenue and Customs (HMRC) formed by merging Inland Revenue with HM Customs and Excise. It will be some years before the two tax systems are fully integrated. In the meantime HMRC is operating like two bodies under one roof. HMRC has some non-tax responsibilities such as administering the national minimum wage and controlling imports.

Tax laws are the longest and most complicated laws passed in the UK. Some taxes have their own Acts of Parliament, such as Value Added Tax Act 1994. Other taxes, such as income tax, have various Acts for different types of income, such as Income Tax (Earnings and Pensions) Act 2003.

Each year, there is a Budget presented by the Chancellor of the Exchequer which makes changes to tax laws. This leads to Finance Acts which have become voluminous since the 1980s.

In addition to Acts of Parliament, tax law is found in:

- statutory instruments, issued by ministers under powers given in an Act;
- extra-statutory concessions issued by HMRC to allow departures from strict tax laws in limited circumstances;
- court cases; and
- decisions of Tax Tribunals (and the bodies that preceded them before 1 April 2009).

HMRC also publishes statements of practices, inspectors' manuals, Revenue Interpretations and other guidance. These give HMRC's understanding of tax law. They do not have the status of law and can be challenged, but HMRC will not question you for following their guidance.

Separate from these national taxes are local authority taxes, namely council tax for individuals and business rates for other bodies.

There is a difference between **tax evasion** and **tax avoidance.** Tax evasion is illegal; it involves submitting false figures or withholding information. Tax avoidance is ordering your affairs to minimise your tax liability within the law. When the Pharisees asked Jesus if they should pay tax to Caesar, he answered "pay unto Caesar what belongs to Caesar" (Matthew 22:21). For the Christian, tax evasion is morally wrong while tax avoidance may not be.

Churches and charities have some special tax provisions. Although often referred to as special provision, in reality churches and charities are often harder hit for tax than commercial businesses, as explained later.

Income tax

Income tax is a charge on the earnings of individuals and partnerships. From 6 April 2005, income tax is used for categories such as employment income and trading income, each with their own rules. Before 6 April 2005, income tax was collected under Schedules, such as Schedule E for employment and Schedule D Case I for trading.

Taxation of profits and surpluses

A church or charity is not liable to income tax or corporation tax on any profit or surplus it makes from charitable activities.

However this exemption does not always apply to any commercial activities which a church undertakes. If a church runs a cafe, sells books, organises concerts or lets rooms, it may find such activities regarded as trading. However there are several exceptions when trading activities escape tax.

Small fund-raising events are exempt from tax under Corporation Tax Act 2010 s483 (previously extra-statutory concession C4). To qualify under this concession:

- the events must not exceed a financial limit (see below);
- the church or charity must not be carrying on the activities as a regular trading event;
- the church or charity must not be competing with other traders; and
- the profits of the activity must be transferred to the church or charity or otherwise applied to charitable purposes.

There are two financial limits. Any event which raises less than £1,000 a week is excluded. Where an event raises more than this, the concession exempts up to 15 of each type of activity in any one location. Events which are exempt from corporation tax under this concession are also exempt from VAT, as explained below.

If s483 does not exempt activities from tax, there was a further tax exemption for small trades under Finance Act 2000 s46. This was repealed in 2010.

Lottery proceeds applied solely to a charity's purposes are exempt under Lotteries and Amusements Act 1976 s3.

Otherwise the **profits from trading** are taxable, even if applied to the church or charity. However this does not always mean you must pay tax. First, many individuals may be involved in selling books or making meals on a voluntary basis. In practice, HMRC allows a reasonable deduction to be made for services provided free. This will reduce the amount of taxable profit, possibly to zero.

Any profit which remain after all these provisions have been considered is subject to corporation tax. However this can easily be avoided by the trading activity setting itself up as a **separate entity**, such as a limited company, and simply donating its profits to the charity under Gift Aid. Donations under Gift Aid are tax deductible as a company expense, so the company pays no tax. Note that to do this:

- a separate legal entity must be created; and
- the company must be registered, have appointed officers, comply with company law, and submit an annual return to Companies House.

Setting up and running a limited company is not onerous, but you must know what you are doing and ensure that you submit your returns on time to avoid paying penalties. A company must have "members" who own the company. Members do not have to be individual people, but must be a "legal person". So a Parochial Church Council of an Anglican church may be the member. From 1 April 2004, a company usually only needs to be audited if its annual turnover exceeds £5.6 million.

Gift Aid

Gift Aid is a scheme whereby donations to a church are made so that the church may recover the tax paid by the donor when earning the money.

The present Gift Aid scheme was introduced on 6 April 2000. It replaces deeds of covenant and the previous Gift Aid scheme introduced in 1990.

The basic rate of income tax is currently 20%. Depending on circumstances, this can mean that a person who earns £100 pays £20 tax and retains £80. Suppose the person donates that £80 to the church under Gift Aid. The church can reclaim the £20 tax paid, in effect increasing his donation to £100.

An extra £20 on top of the £80 donation is an increase of 25%. So Gift Aid is a simple means by which a church can increase this income by a quarter.

The main points to note are:

- tax may only be reclaimed by a church or a registered charity, not by an unregistered body;
- the church or charity must register with HMRC, and will be given a charity reference number;
- the church or charity must appoint one person as the "authorised official" to reclaim the tax;
- a donor may only use Gift Aid if the donor pays income tax. Non-taxpayers should not use Gift Aid;
- Gift Aid may not be used to reclaim tax on donations made from an account where tax has already been refunded, such as a CAF payment;
- the donor signs a Gift Aid declaration, allowing the church or charity to recover tax for any or all donations made from 6 April 2000 (provided the donor was a taxpayer when the donation was made);
- the authorised official completes claim form R68 periodically and sends it to HMRC who refunds tax.

The Gift Aid declaration is not an official form, so the church may design its own forms, and have different forms for different purposes. The only information a donor needs to give is their name and address. Regular donors may complete a form which can easily be produced on a single sheet of paper. People seeking sponsorship may produce a form listing the names and addresses of sponsors with the amount donated. For occasional donors, such as cathedral visitors, the declaration can be printed on the gift envelope. The HMRC website contains sample declaration forms.

Before 6 April 2008, the basic rate of income tax was 22% which was the equivalent of more than 28% gross. For a transitional period of three years to 5 April 2011, HMRC refunded income tax at the higher rate.

Operation of Gift Aid

Gift Aid may only be used to reclaim sums paid to a church or a registered charity. It should only be used by donors who are taxpayers. A new charity must be registered before it may use Gift Aid (see chapter 10). The scheme was introduced on 6 April 2000.

The taxpayer must keep a record of all donations made using Gift Aid, as this must be disclosed on the tax return.

Donors who do not pay tax should not use Gift Aid. In some cases, a taxpayer may make a donation from tax paid in the previous tax year.

Information about Gift Aid is freely available on the HMRC website at http://www.inlandrevenue.gov.uk/charities. This website also contains copies of forms which may be downloaded.

Every church or charity which uses Gift Aid must appoint an **authorised official** to deal with HMRC. This may be the Treasurer or it may be another officer, such as a stewardship secretary. That is a matter for the church itself to decide.

The form requires this information about the authorised official:

- name;
- national insurance number;
- day-time telephone number (optional but desirable);
- church address;
- address to send repayments.

The form must be countersigned by a second church officer, such as a minister, elder or churchwarden.

Every church and charity is given a charity reference number by HMRC. This must be quoted on all claim forms and correspondence.

The claim from HMRC is made on claim form R68. For security reasons, this must be obtained direct from HMRC. The website contains a specimen form so you can see what it looks like, but you may not use a downloaded form to make claims.

Higher rate taxpayers and Gift Aid

Suppose a basic rate taxpayer gives £100 to a church under Gift Aid. He has earned £125 before tax to have £100 after tax; 20% of £125 is £25. This means that he gives the church £100, and the church can reclaim £25.

Some taxpayers are liable to pay tax at the higher rate of 40% or additional rate of 50%. Suppose a higher rate taxpayer gives

£100 to the church under Gift Aid. The Gift Aid system does not know who pays tax at higher rate, and so it allows the church still to reclaim £25 on the donor's earnings of £125. However a donor has paid tax of 40% of £125 which is £50. So HMRC refunds the extra £25 *to the taxpayer*, not to the church.

A taxpayer paying income tax at the additional rate of 50%, pays £62.50 tax on £125. So HMRC refunds the extra £37.50 to the taxpayer.

It should be noted that the 2011 Budget included provisions to simplify the paperwork for Gift Aid.

Payroll giving

An alternative tax-effective method of giving to charity is payroll giving, also known as Give As You Earn (GAYE). From 6 April 2000, this may be used to make donations of any amount. Before that date there was an annual maximum of £1,200 per employee per year.

The scheme is optional to all parties. Payroll giving may only be operated if there is agreement by:

• the employer to run a scheme (which must be registered with HMRC);
• the employee to make donations; and
• an agency to accept donations and pass them to whatever charity the employee chooses.

The main agencies are:

• Achisomoch Aid Company
• BEN – Motor and Allied Trades Benevolent Fund
• Charities Aid Foundation
• Charities Trust
• The Charity Service Ltd
• KKL Payroll Giving Agency
• Northern Ireland Council for Voluntary Action
• Scottish Council for Voluntary Organisations
• Charitable Giving
• Stewardship Payroll Giving
• United Way Payroll Giving Service
• The Lincolnshire Community Foundation
• H-PAN

Payroll giving allows an employee to have part of his pay deducted at source by the employer and passed to a church or charity. The employer deducts the donation from *gross pay* which has the effect of reducing the amount of the employee's net pay. This means that *the employee gets all the benefit of the tax relief* and the charity gets none.

Suppose an employee earns £2,000 a month and pays tax of £300. The employee decided to give £100 a month to the parish church. This reduces the employee's gross pay to £1,900 and reduces the tax to £280. Note that the church receives just £100 and cannot reclaim any tax as under Gift Aid. The employee receives the whole of the benefit of the £20 saved tax.

Larger savings may be made by taxpayers subject to higher rates.

VAT on trading activities

A church or charity has no general exemption from value added tax (VAT) as it has from corporation tax. In general, a church or charity must pay VAT on its purchases, and may be required to charge VAT on supplies it makes while trading.

If a charity trades, it can be required to charge VAT on its supplies if:

- the annual turnover exceeds the registration limit;
- the income from trading activities exceeds those for the corporation tax exemption;
- the trading activities come within the scope of a "business"; and
- the supplies are subject to VAT.

The **registration limit** is revised each year in the Budget with effect from 1 April. The limit from 1 April 2011 is £73,000. Note that this limit only applies to *business* income, not other income. If your business income is less than this limit, you do not need to register for VAT, though you may register voluntarily.

If your income from trading activities does meet the corporation tax rules given above for **small fund-raising events** (no more than 15 per year, ignoring those below £1,000 a week), those events are exempt from VAT. However note that there is no VAT exemption for **small trades** as there is for corporation tax.

VAT may only be charged for a **business activity.** There is no exact definition of what constitutes a business activity and there have been several cases in marginal areas. In general a business activity involves:

- selling goods or services;
- doing so with reasonable frequency; and
- doing so for a reasonable period.

An activity can be a business activity even though the price simply covers the cost of the supply. Also, a single event, such as a concert, can be regarded as a business supply.

The following activities are definitely *not* business activities:

- receiving voluntary donations;
- worship;
- receipt of a legacy;
- dealing in shares by a charity.

The following activities are business activities:

- compulsory admission charges;
- sales of goods (including donated goods);
- building hire; and
- exports of goods outside the European Union.

The following activities are only non-business if conditions are met:

- advertisements in charity brochures, provided at least 50% are from individuals who are not advertising a trade;
- welfare services, where the charge is at least 15% below cost;
- catering, if ancillary to a welfare service;
- sponsorship, if the sponsor receives nothing in return (in which case it is not really sponsorship at all);
- secondment of staff, if the staff are seconded to the charitable activities of another charity; and
- membership subscriptions, unless the member receives no more in return than the right to receive reports and take part in management.

16

Specific Denominations

This section gives some further advice about specific denominations.

Baptish Church

Baptist Churches are managed by trusts, one of:

- the Baptist Union Corporation
- a local Baptist Trust Corporation, or
- individuals.

The Baptist Union Corporation was founded in the 1890s to overcome problems of having individual trustees, and having to trace each individual for many transactions such as a sale of land. The Baptist and Congregational Trusts Act 1951 allows the Baptist Union Corporation or a regional Trust Corporation (but not a trust of individuals) to use a model trust. The latest versions are called Baptist Trusts and were made available from 2 May 2003. Previous versions were called Fuller Trusts or Fairbairn Trusts. When these trusts are adopted they prevail over the original trust (known as the foundation trust) except for some specific matters such as doctrine and qualification of ministers where the foundation trust prevails.

These trustees are called **holding trustees** because they hold the church building for the benefit of church members. The local church has **managing trustees** who look after the day-to-day running of the church. The managing trustees are usually the minister and diaconate. Local churches are almost entirely self-governing and autonomous.

The appointment of a treasurer is a matter for the local church. Some have a policy that the treasurer must be appointed from the diaconate. A treasurer appointed outside the diaconate automatically becomes a deacon on appointment. It is up to the local church whether to appoint the treasurer for one year at a time or for a longer period, and whether to have a finance committee.

The auditor or examiner must be independent. Guidance from the church states that person must "have no connection with the deacons". This means that the auditor or examiner mist not be a deacon, nor a close relative, business partner or employee of a deacon, or be a person who makes "very large donations" to the church. "Subject to these provisos, a church member may serve as an independent examiner provided he or she has the requisite ability and practical experience and has not served as a deacon during, or since, the accounting period under review".

The Baptist Union Corporation encourages Baptist churches to give at least 5% of their income to the work of BMS World Mission and Home Mission Front.

The minister is employed by the local church, so the treasurer is expected to pay the minister, including operating a PAYE payroll for him. The treasurer is also expected to pay visiting preachers.

The Baptist Union Corporation produces detailed guidelines on many aspects of accounts. These can be accessed from www.baptist.org.uk.

Church of England

The Church of England is the established church in England. It comprises the two provinces of Canterbury and York which between them are divided into 43 dioceses plus the Diocese in Europe. Dioceses are divided into deaneries which comprise about 16,000 parishes, some of which are held in groups.

The treasurer is appointed by the parochial church council (PCC), which may appoint joint treasurers. If no treasurer is appointed, the churchwardens must act as treasurer. The treasurer must be a member of the PCC, but as PCCs have a power to co-opt members, a suitable non-member can easily be made a PCC member. The treasurer must not be paid for his services. The treasurer may also be the PCC secretary, though this is discouraged.

The annual general meeting appoints the auditor or examiner, failing which the PCC may appoint someone. That person may not be a PCC member.

The decisions about funds are the responsibility of the PCC

which is elected by the annual general meeting apart from some ex-officio members, such as the minister and the parish's deanery synod members. Every parish must keep a register of services which records, among other matters, the amount of offertory taken at individual services. Under the PCCs (Powers) Measure 1956, PCCs are trustees of income and expenditure but not necessarily of the church's assets.

The Church of England has its own laws and its own courts to enforce these laws. These include the Church Accounting Regulations 1997 to 2001 which are obligatory on parishes. Accounts must be made up for calendar years ending on 31 December. The PCC must consider them before they are presented to the annual meeting. The accounts must be displayed on a notice board for at least seven days before the annual meeting.

The church and parsonage is legally owned by the incumbent (vicar or rector), making most of them millionaires (in theory). In practice, all the usual rights of ownership are vested in other bodies. The parsonage is usually managed by a diocesan parsonage board.

Ministers of the Church of England are paid centrally, though the parish is expected to reimburse the minister's expenses, such as travel and telephone.

Curates and assistant clergy are also employed and paid centrally (though some assistant clergy are now unpaid, combining their office with secular employment). The parish usually provides accommodation for the curate, and is expected to pay the curate's expenses.

The parish is required to make a contribution to the diocese, known as diocesan quota or parish share. This can be the largest single expense in a parish's accounts. Although not legally enforceable, parishes generally pay it. The funds are used to pay the minister, pay for his parsonage, fund the minister's pension and train clergy, among other general expenses.

The parish is expected to pay for the maintenance of the church building, and for the employment of any staff other than ministers. Some canons impose particular obligations on the parish. For example, canon F5 requires the parish to provide and maintain surplices for the minister, and canon F13 requires the church to be properly maintained. Canon F17 requires a register to be kept of church property. Separate law requires churches to be professionally surveyed every five years.

There is no obligation on the church to support charities but canon F10 requires every church to have an alms box for distribution as the minister and PCC see fit. The church may support charities whose objects are consistent with advancing the mission of the church.

The Central Board of Finance of the Church operates the CBF Church of England Investment Fund. This is a managed collective investment scheme in which Church of England parishes and other bodies may invest their funds. It has an ethical investment policy and has consistently achieved above-average returns on investments.

Church of Scotland

The Church of Scotland, commonly known as the Kirk, is the established church in Scotland. It was formed in 1560. Unlike its English equivalent, it does not regard itself as a state church and jealously protects itself from state involvement. It is Presbyterian and not Episcopalian by nature, and is therefore not simply a Scottish version of the Church of England.

The central body has various funds to help individual churches, and also provides resources for individual churches.

Every congregation in the Church of Scotland is allocated the sum it is to contribute to the National Stipend Fund and to the Mission and Renewal Fund. These allocations are based on the congregations' incomes.

Methodist Church

Each local Methodist church is a separate charity with excepted status (see page 97). The church council comprises its **managing trustees**. There are separate managing trustees for circuits and districts. Local churches are expected to make contributions to the circuit.

Every Methodist church must complete a document known as Schedule B. This is a summary of the church accounts. It is sent via the circuit to the Connexional Property Committee based in Manchester.

The church treasurer is appointed by the local church council and must be a member of the Methodist Church. The responsibility for the funds rests with the church council. All cheques must have two signatures. The collections must be counted by two people and details entered on an **offerings record.**

Roman Catholic Church

In the Roman Catholic Church, each diocese is a separate excepted charity. Each parish is a branch of that charity. The diocese states what information it wishes to receive from the parish.

United Reformed Church (URC)

The United Reformed Church was formed in 1972 by a merger of Congregational and Presbyterian churches. The Re-formed Association of Churches of Christ joined in 1981, and the Congregational Union of Scotland joined in April 2000. The URC has 1,750 congregations served by 1,100 ministers.

Its main authoritative body is the annual General Assembly attended by 700 delegates which determines general policy, implemented by committees of the Assembly. A Moderator, lay or ordained, is elected each year.

The treasurer is appointed by the Church Meeting on the recommendation of the Elders' Meeting. The treasurer is accountable to both meetings, though individual churches usually agree one in practice. The treasurer may be an elder, which the URC official policy regards as 'helpful'.

Bank signatories include the treasurer and whatever other signatories the Church Meeting approves, often on the recommendation of the treasurer.

The church may have a finance committee, in which case the treasurer should automatically be appointed a member. The URC policy is that a church should have a finance committee if there are sufficient people to serve on it.

The URC defines the job of treasurer as:

- ensuring collection of all church income
- paying all expenses authorized by the Church Meeting
- recording all transactions
- reporting
- preparing a budget.

The first of these tasks may be delegated.

The duty to report includes not just an income and expense account, but also a statement of assets and liabilities (broadly, a balance sheet).

It is recommended that the treasurer should not record members' freewill offerings nor reclaim tax under Gift Aid. URC has its own guidance on Gift Aid.

The URC has district treasurers who are available to help church treasurers and produces a guidance Plan for Partnership in Ministerial Training which explains what expenses it considers appropriate for the minister to claim. This is available from the Finance Office at Tavistock Place, or from the URC website. The Church operates a freewill offering (FWO) scheme of envelopes. The central Finance Office provides resources under the name The Responsibility Is Ours (TRIO).

17

Stewardship

Introduction

Stewardship is when church members give a share of their time, talents and money to the work of the church. The traditional gift was the tithe, or one-tenth. There are many references to tithes in the Old Testament, such as Leviticus 27.30, 32: 'Every tithe on land, whether from grain or from the fruit of a tree, belongs to the Lord; it is holy to the Lord . . . Every tenth creature that passes under the counting rod is holy to the Lord; this applies to all tithes of cattle and sheep. '

This Old Testament practice is obliquely upheld by Jesus in Matthew 23.23: 'Alas for you, scribes and Pharisees, hypocrites! You pay tithes of mint and dill and cummin, but you have overlooked the weightier demands of the law – justice, mercy, and good faith. It is these you should have practised, *without neglecting the others*.' These final words indicate that tithes should still be paid, although there are other virtues that Christians should practise.

Christians today debate whether 10% is still an appropriate figure based just on an oblique Gospel reference to Old Testament law. If so, does the 10% apply to income before or after tax, and after any expenses?

Some Christians observe that the Old Testament tithe provided much benefit which is now centrally funded from tax and national insurance, charged at rates much higher than 10%. Accordingly, it is argued, a lower percentage than 10% is justified. The Church of England has set a target of 5% of take-home pay. The answer is in 2 Corinthians 9.7: 'Each person should give as he has decided for himself; there should be no reluctance, no sense of compulsion; God loves a cheerful giver.'

Charitable donations

It is common for churches not only to receive gifts under stewardship, but also to make gifts. Many churches have a policy of
giving away 10% of income. A church which has such a policy
should ensure that it is sufficiently precise.

What income is included?

A church has many sources of income. It needs to define which
ones are included in the 10% policy. Here is a typical list with
the author's suggestions of whether each one should be included.
This is simply a suggestion. Each church is free to make its policy
as it wishes.

Whether income should be included in charitable reckoning

Source of income	Yes or no
Regular giving	Yes
Casual giving (cash collection)	Yes
Tax recovered on giving	Yes
Legacies	No
Funds raised for a specific purpose	No
Income from trading activities*	Yes
Interest on deposits and investments	Yes
Payment of insurance claims	No
Expenses refunded, or loans repaid	No

* You may wish to include profit from such activities

How do you time payments?

The policy must establish to which year's income the percentage
is to be applied, and how the payments should be made. A simple
policy is to apply the percentage to the previous year's income
as the amount is then known at the start of the year. Payments
can be made in twelve equal monthly instalments, or however the
church wishes to make them.

Scams

Sadly, there are scams which seek to exploit churches' compassion with false claims. These can range from professional beggars on the street to bogus letters from penniless students in Africa.

Outside local need, Christian compassion can be met by giving to reputable agencies. Organizations such as Crisis and the Salvation Army have vast experience in meeting such needs efficiently.

Begging letters from Africa may ask for funds in emotional terms, such as to help a child to receive medicine or education. A good response is to ask for the name of the hospital or college, and then ask church authorities out there to check that it exists. It may be possible to make payment to the overseas church and for them to pay the payment direct. However, if using an overseas church in this way, make a donation to them also. It is unreasonable to expect overseas churches to provide free banking and credit reference services.

If you write letters to the person and send a personal cheque, you have provided specimen signatures and all the details to access your account. It is then a simple matter to forge documents to transfer funds from your account. Sometimes the fraudster may justify such action by saying that we in the West are only wealthy at their expense. Whatever your views on such matters, they do not justify theft. Your responsibility as treasurer and as an individual Christian is to look after the funds entrusted to your care.

Policy for supporting individuals overseas:

- make payments to established bodies, rather than individuals
- ask the local church authorities to check the body concerned
- make payments in small instalments and ask for evidence of how they are being used
- do not use your normal signature in any letters
- transfer funds into a bank account opened for that purpose, and only keep in it sufficient funds to cover the payments from it.

18

Audit and Examination

Introduction

Accounts must either be audited or examined depending on the size of the church. A church eligible for external examination may choose a full audit instead. For financial periods that end after 31 March 2009, a church with either gross expenditure or gross income exceeding £500,000 must have the accounts audited by a professional auditor. If the gross income is between £250,000 and £500,000, the law requires that the accounts have an independent examination by a qualified accountant. Below the figure of £250,000, the accounts must have an independent examination, but the examiner need not be a qualified accountant. These requirements are imposed by the Charity Commission.

An audit or examination is not designed to see if the treasurer is funnelling the church funds into his secret Swiss bank account. The purpose is to add credibility to the treasurer's work. It has the nature of a second opinion. It allows for the possibility that the treasurer may have made a mistake or could present some figures more clearly. It reaffirms the competence and value of the treasurer.

In the unlikely event that the examiner or auditor does discover a serious concern, the examiner and auditor must raise that promptly with the appropriate church authorities and reflect it in the audit report. In some instances, the examiner or auditor may be required to report a discrepancy to another authority, usually the Charity Commission.

The treasurer must fully co-operate with the auditor or examiner. A treasurer should not seek to influence what the auditor or examiner reports, nor should the treasurer be obstructive in making records available and providing explanations. To be obstructive not only defeats the purpose of the audit or examination, but can be a criminal offence in extreme cases.

Independent examiner

For examination, the church must appoint an independent examiner. This need not be a qualified accountant but must be someone who has 'the requisite ability and practical experience to carry out a competent examination of the accounts'. Although requisite ability and practical experience have not been further defined, it is regarded that the person must have some book-keeping skills and some familiarity with church affairs. Even a person with such knowledge and skill may need further advice, particularly on the charities SORP and other relevant accounting standards.

'Independent' means that the person must not be:

- a member of the church council, diaconate, trustees or equivalent body, or any of its sub-committees, though the examiner may be a member of the church
- employed by the church or receive any fees from the church (other than as independent examiner)
- a close relative of someone who is within the two categories above.

It is important to bear in mind that the youth leader's father or the churchwarden's wife are not eligible.

The church may pay a fee and expenses to the independent examiner. The appointment should be confirmed in a letter.

The church should not just appoint the first person willing to do the job, but should satisfy itself that the person is competent. If necessary, ask to see a CV (career details), interview the person and take up references. The church does this for other senior offices (or should do). Anyone who recommends someone should be asked what knowledge they have of their nominee. There have been cases where a church member has recommended someone who does not even exist.

Independent examination

An independent examination is much less comprehensive than an audit. If church members are unhappy about this, they should vote for a full audit.

Functions that are included in an audit but not an independent examination include:

- whether the accounts are 'true and fair'
- whether records are properly kept rather than just whether there may be evidence of a major failure
- substantive testing of accounting procedures
- full checking of post-balance sheet events.

The duties of the independent examiner are to:

- check that the church is below the threshold for a full audit
- examine the accounting records
- compare those records to the published accounts
- consider disclosures
- consider any unusual items.

And that is it. Unless the examiner is following up a suspicion, the examiner does not check entries against vouchers, or that expenditure has been properly incurred, or that all cash has been banked.

To do the job properly, the independent examiner should:

- understand the church structure
- understand the treasurer's accounting system
- read the minutes of the church council or equivalent body to gain an understanding of the issues involved and objectives
- make some test checks, following records through the audit trail (see page 17) though not usually to vouchers or source documents
- consider the bank reconciliations (see page 49)
- compare this year's figures with the previous year and seek explanations for significant variances
- consider whether sources of income are consistent with known sources
- consider the reasonableness of any estimate or other assumption
- ensure that accounts have been prepared on a consistent basis

- check that any statements in the treasurer's report or any other report are consistent with the accounts.

Independent examiner's report

The independent examiner must feel free to report whatever he believes needs to be reported, regardless of the sensitivies or consequences of the report.

An **unqualified report** may read:

> In connection with my examination, no matter has come to my attention:
> (1) which gives me reasonable cause to believe that in any material respect the requirements
> - to keep accounting records in accordance with section 41 of the Charities Act 1993; and
> - to prepare accounts which accord with the accounting records and comply with the requirements of the Act and the Regulations have not been met; or
> (2) to which, in my opinion, attention should be drawn in order to enable a proper understanding of the accounts to be reached.

Signature, name, address and date.

A **qualified report** will either identify a concern or give information which has been omitted.

An example of the former is: 'The incumbent and church council refused to provide me details of a separately administered charity called [whatever] and administered for the benefit of the church. This gives me reasonable cause to believe that in this respect the accounts do not comply with the accounting requirements of the Act.'

An example of the latter is: 'The accounts do not record the gift of £5,000 from the Friends of Lower Snoddington to pay for a youth worker.'

In most cases such sentences are put in front of the wording of the unqualified report, and the next sentence starts, 'Apart from this matter . . .'

Audit

The audit is a more thorough process, but the church members should still not assume that the audit automatically confirms the accuracy and reliability of the accounting records. The audit simply provides a level of assurance that the accounts are true and fair, and accord with the accounting records.

An audit may be done only by a qualified accountant (see page 95). Such an accountant is provided with all auditing guidelines and standards by his professional body and so the details are not reproduced here.

An audit report may be qualified or unqualified in the same way as an independent examiner's report.

19

Miscellaneous

Risk assessment

Charities are expected to conduct a risk assessment on all aspects of their work, not just financial. A risk has been defined as 'the threat that an event or action will adversely affect an organization's ability to achieve its objectives and execute its strategies'.

A risk assessment is a thorough review of all the church's work. This should involve all church officers, who may be assisted by outside bodies. A church and its members will have performed much risk assessment instinctively.

The types of risk to identify are:

- financial risk, the commonest form
- reputational risk, such as adverse publicity
- statutory and legal requirements, such as not complying with child protection procedures
- operational risk, such as damage to church premises.

The process in outline can be summarized as:

- identify the church's core activities
- ask each church group to identify risks they face
- identify what statutory considerations apply in that area
- collate the risks
- assess the risks according to likelihood and impact
- identify controls to minimize risks and their consequences.

High impact means that the consequence could be devastating, such as if a child was run over in the church car park. High likelihood means that a risk could happen but may not have much impact, such as dropping a pile of hymn books.

Risks can be tabulated according to likelihood and impact, and action determined thus as in

Figure 10: Risks

	Low likelihood (not expected to happen)	Medium likelihood (could happen)	High likelihood (expected to happen)
High impact	Establish contingency plans and preventive controls.	Take steps to reduce likelihood and establish contingency plans.	Take immediate steps to reduce likelihood.
Medium impact	Accept risk. Respond if threat occurs.	Establish contingency plans and preventive controls.	Take steps to reduce likelihood and establish contingency plans.
Low impact	Accept the risk.	Accept risk. Respond if threat occurs.	Establish contingency plans and preventive controls.

In each case, you should consider how far insurance is appropriate.

Risk is addressed in three ways:

- prevent the risk happening
- limit the consequences of the risk
- protect against consequences of risk.

Consider the risk of fire. This can be addressed in these three ways by:

- not using naked flames, removing flammable material, checking electrical wiring
- having fire extinguishers, keeping fire doors closed, using fire-retardant materials
- having insurance cover for fire.

Personal debt problems

A church may be asked to help a person with personal financial problems. This may take the form of someone knocking on the vicarage door to a request to the treasurer for some financial advice. The church should have clear policies in these areas. The church should combine a soft heart with a hard head. Shrewdness and discernment are as much Christian characteristics as generosity. To give money to fraudsters is mis-stewardship of resources and helps fund crime.

Requests for help should be met in kind, not cash. Where a church is regularly asked for help by the hungry, it should consider having a larder scheme or luncheon club where these needs can be met. It is advisable to set up such a scheme in conjunction with other local churches and possibly other religious groups and secular charities. You may be able to agree a division of responsibilities between you. When a minister provides relief, the church should be willing to refund this as an expense.

For local need, such as beggars on the street, a simple policy is always to make donations in kind. Give people food rather than money to buy food. If possible, stay with them while they eat it. The scriptures talk of meeting need, but nowhere says to give money directly to those affected. Even the Good Samaritan did not give money to the victim (whose honesty is not questioned) but paid the innkeeper direct, and offered to make a second trip to settle any further costs (Luke 10.35). Jesus concludes with the words 'Go and do as he did.' Money can be used to buy liquor, drugs or meths but food can only be eaten. The author's experience is that fewer than one in four beggars takes up an offer of free food.

Some churches give the minister a **discretionary fund** to meet personal needs as the minister sees fit. This is a worthy aim of a church but needs control. Suggested controls are:

- the minister avoids handing over cash but instead provides goods or help in kind or pays a bill for the person
- financial help should always be part of pastoral help as financial problems rarely occur outside other difficulties. The minister should seek to help the person with the underlying and consequential problems and should seek to pray with the person
- while respecting confidentiality, at least one other person

should know of all donations. The church council should nominate that person. It may be the treasurer, auditor, church-warden, or senior deacon. This allows the minister an opportunity to discuss difficult cases and protects the minister against any accusation of misuse of funds

- the minister should keep a record of all such help provided
- the minister should be prepared to refer a person in difficulties to an outside agency who may be able to provide particular help.

A church or minister should never lend money. If you really believe that a financial need can only be met by providing cash, it must always be as a gift. A loan in such circumstances will probably not be repayable and this creates new problems, such as the person feeling he cannot come back for further help. When a person is restored to prosperity, there is no problem in his making a gift to the church in recognition of the help once received.

A very common problem now is **personal debt,** because of the sophistication of modern marketing methods and a lack of understanding by consumers. For example, few people realize that paying 75p per £100 to protect your credit card balance against being unable to pay means that over forty years you have paid a premium of £120 to insure £100 against an eventuality that never happens. Income protection plans are available much less expensively from reputable insurance companies.

Personal debt problems are so common, it is almost certain that your church includes many people in that position, including senior officers, perhaps even the minister. As a church treasurer you may be approached for debt advice because of your standing and financial knowledge. Do not refuse such a request, as you may be the only person asked, and a refusal could discourage a person from seeking the help they need. It is reasonable to point out that others may be better able to help, but never refuse help yourself. If you feel inadequate to the task, that is probably a good sign; it makes it easier for God to work through you.

Some basic points about recovering from debt are noted below. It should be remembered that this is only a general framework which needs adaptation for an individual's personal circumstances.

General advice on recovering from personal debt

1 Do not consolidate debts, however much you enjoy the television advertisements suggesting you should. Consolidation incurs extra expense and means that the debtor loses control

2 Seek help from a free debt advice agency. Never pay for this service. Keep the debtor calm and restrain dramatic gestures. Always generate hope. Remember to pray

3 Cancel all inessential expenditure. This includes all savings plans (including insurance-based ones), subscriptions, book clubs and similar. If there are any endowments or other savings, seek advice on whether it is worth cashing them in. But don't become a martyr. No one gets out of debt by living on economy baked beans and not switching on lights at night

4 Identify any underlying problem and deal with it. The problem may be drink, gambling, compulsive spending or a host of other issues. Unless financial problems arise from a failed business venture, there is always an underlying cause

5 If the debtor has a mortgage, it may be possible to extend the period, consolidate some of the debts into the mortgage, and pay interest only for a while. However, such decisions should be made on professional advice and the particular circumstances

6 Cut up all credit cards. Use cash or a debit card. If the bank is being difficult, close the account and regard the overdraft as another creditor. Open another account

7 List all the debts; and this means *all* the debts. Debtors can be very reluctant to admit the whole list and will often exclude such items as personal loans from friends and family. Such debts may be non-urgent, but they are still debts. Listing all debts means opening every envelope

8 Analyse income from all sources and necessary living expenditure to see what funds are available to clear debts.

This, again, is an area where total honesty comes at a premium

9 Be reluctant to move to a smaller house to release capital. The expenses of estate agents, solicitors, removal expenses and stamp duty land tax can easily consume all that capital. A decision to move or take equity release should be made on professional advice. The local authority may have a mortgage rescue scheme which can help

10 Check that the debtor is receiving all tax reliefs and social security benefits to which he or she is entitled. Excellent advice on welfare benefits can be obtained from Child Poverty Action Group and Citizens' Advice Bureaux. There may be local charities which can help. See if any inessential possessions could reasonably be sold for a reasonable figure. Identify opportunities for additional earnings

11 Do not let the debtor be harassed by creditors. It is reasonable for them to chase up debts, but harassing a debtor is a criminal offence. Do not ignore anything from a court

12 Sort out priority debts and pay them first. These are all taxes, most hire purchase, fines, electricity and gas (not water), maintenance and child support, rent, mortgage and television licence. Don't pay any other bills until priority debts are up to date

13 List credit card bills and other interest-charging bills according to the interest rate charged. Pay off the monthly minimum on all credit cards except that with the highest interest, where as much as possible is paid. Store cards usually have the highest interest rates

14 For other creditors, write explaining how the debt will be cleared even if only at the rate of £1 a month. You don't ask the creditors, you tell them. It is often a pleasant surprise how reasonable creditors become when they realize that the only alternative is receiving nothing. The debtor may be terribly embarrassed by all this, but no one else will be

15 If the situation is so hopeless that these plans cannot re-solve the matter, consider an individual voluntary agree-ment (IVA) with creditors or even bankruptcy. But such a step should only be taken as a last resort with profes-sional advice and personal support

Confidentiality

A church treasurer will receive much confidential information. Common examples include how much particular church mem-bers give, instances where church members have been helped financially, and legal and commercial negotiations where disclo-sure of information could prejudice the outcome. As the church treasurer is a senior church officer, the treasurer may often learn of sensitive non-financial matters.

Broadly, information can be classified into three levels of con-fidentiality:

• public information
• legal and commercial information
• personal information.

In a church, all information should be publicly available unless there is a good reason for it not to be. Within reason, a church treasurer should answer questions and divulge figures unless it comes within the scope of confidentiality. A church treasurer should not only answer questions if satisfied that the person needs to know. Although churches are not covered by the Freedom of Information Act, they should act as though they are.

Legal and commercial information may need to be withheld while negotiations are pending. Premature release of quotations for building work could affect the quotations received from other builders, for example. Here confidentiality usually means postponing disclosure until a case has been settled or a contract signed. Legal and commercial sensitivity rarely justifies indefinite suppression.

Personal information relates to identifiable individuals. If those individuals are prepared to disclose information involving them, that is their decision. They may also authorize you to disclose that information generally or to a specific third party, such as when a church employee needs confirmation of earnings. Otherwise, regard such personal information as confidential indefinitely.

Be careful in publishing summary information, such as how many individuals contribute more than £500 a year to the church, and how many are over 60. It is surprising how little analysis need be published before individuals can be identified.

There are some statutory exceptions where information must be disclosed regardless of whether the other parties agree. These are:

- evidence of treason, terrorism, drug trafficking or money laundering
- suspicion (not just evidence) of money laundering
- payroll information about an employee to the tax authorities
- any information required by a court order
- certain information required by an insolvency practitioner about a bankrupt.

Accountants, auditors, treasurers and similar office holders are not generally obliged to disclose evidence of other crimes, such as theft or tax evasion. Professional guidance to qualified accountants indicates that they should only make such disclosure if 'in the public interest'. This involves considering:

- the relative size of the sums involved and the extent of any financial damage
- whether members of the public are likely to be affected
- the likelihood of repetition
- the reasons why the individual will not disclose the matter himself
- the gravity of the offence
- relevant legislation and accounting standards
- any legal advice obtained.

Any such disclosure is always a serious step. The treasurer should seek advice from a qualified accountant or lawyer in most cases before making such disclosure.

If a treasurer is accused of any malpractice, the treasurer is released from any duty of confidentiality to the minimum extent necessary to defend himself.

Miscellaneous

Legal tender

Legal tender comprises the following coins issued by the Royal Mint from the year stated:

Coin	First issued
1p	1971
2p	1971
5p	1990
10p	1992
20p	1982
50p	1997
£1	1983
£2	1998

and the following bank notes issued by the Bank of England:

Note	First issued
£50	1994 and 2011
£20	2007
£10	2000
£5	2002

In addition, the following rare coins are also legal tender:

- Britannia gold coins minted from 1987 for £100, £50, £25 and £10
- £5 and £2 gold coins minted from 1887
- sovereigns (£1) and half-sovereigns (50p) from 1838
- commemorative £5 coins minted from 1990
- commemorative £2 coins minted in 1986, 1989, 1994, 1995 and 1996
- commemorative crowns (25p) between 1816 and 1981
- double florins (20p) minted between 1887 and 1890
- Maundy money for 1p, 2p, 3p and 4p (even if minted before decimalization in 1971).

Should you find any of this last list of coins in the collection, you may be better advised selling them to a coin dealer.

In practice, any cheques or postal orders made out to the church are also included.

There are three **Scottish** banks and four Northern **Irish** banks which are still allowed to issue their own notes. The Scottish banks are Bank of Scotland, Royal Bank of Scotland and Clydesdale

Bank. The Irish banks are Allied Irish Bank (also known as First Trust Bank), Bank of Ireland, Northern Bank, Ulster Bank. They each produce £5, £10, £20 and £100 notes. Bank of Scotland also produces £1 notes, and two Irish banks produce £50 notes. These notes are not strictly speaking legal tender anywhere, not even in Scotland or Ireland, though UK banks accept them.

Old bank notes never lose their value and may be exchanged at the Bank of England for their face value. Sometimes old notes are worth more to collectors. Old coins may be exchanged for value at the Royal Mint if provided in at least £1 of each coin.

Foreign notes and coins are not legal tender. Notes may be exchanged at main banks and post offices for UK currency which may then be added to the collection. Coins cannot be exchanged, but may be offered to the congregation who may be willing to buy them for UK currency.

Forged notes and coins are not worth anything. It is not an offence to keep a forgery, but it is an offence to sell it for less than the face value. There are several ways to check notes, but the Bank of England recommends four simple tests:

1 feel of the paper: it should be crisp, and slightly rough in the heavily printed areas. It should not be limp, waxy or shiny
2 watermark: should be hardly apparent until held up to the light. The mark is a clearly defined portrait of the Queen, with gradations of light and shade
3 thread: genuine notes have a stardust thread which looks like a dotted silver line which becomes solid when held to the light
4 printing: lines are clear and not soft or fuzzy. The colours are pure and clear. The words 'Bank of England' are raised, which can be felt by running a thumb over the words.

Insolvency

Insolvency is an inability to pay one's debts as they fall due. In itself this is purely a financial situation with no legal consequences.

There are various arrangements which provide a measure of protection for both individuals and organizations. These include the ability to make individual voluntary arrangements (IVAs) for individuals and company voluntary arrangements (CVAs) for companies. An IVA or CVA creates a moratorium in which legal proceedings may not be started to recover a debt. It allows the person or business to come to an agreement with creditors to clear arrears. There are other ways of achieving this.

An individual may become bankrupt. Under new laws introduced from 1 April 2004, this imposes restrictions on that individual for between one year and fifteen years. An insolvency practitioner is appointed as trustee in bankruptcy to seize such property as can be found to sell for the benefit of creditors. The bankrupt is then discharged, with any unpaid debts extinguished.

A company may go into **administration**, which means it continues in business under the management of an insolvency practitioner. It may go into **receivership**, which means that some bits of it may be continued while others are wound up. Or it may go into **liquidation**, which means it is wound up and ceases to exist.

In bankruptcy or liquidation, such funds as may be obtained by the insolvency practitioner are generally distributed to various classes of creditor in this order:

- pre-preferential debts (expenses of liquidator)
- preferential debts (mainly staff wages to a limit)
- secured creditors (typically banks who have provided loans)
- unsecured creditors (trade suppliers)
- shareholders or members.

Each class must have all their debts paid before any debt is paid for the next class, except that from 15 September 2003 some assets must be reserved for unsecured creditors. The amount which must be reserved depends on the amount of realized assets:

Realized assets	*Available for unsecured creditors*
To £10,000	Half the realized assets
Over £10,000	£5,000 plus 20% of the excess above £10,000 to a maximum of £600,000.

This explanation helps the treasurer explain what happens if you have the misfortune of a debtor becoming insolvent. You will probably receive a proportion of the money owed to you and have to write off the rest.

It is possible for a church or charity to become insolvent. A Church of England parish or cathedral cannot be bankrupted. In 2003, Blackburn Cathedral lost £4.5 million in an unsuccessful millennium exhibition. In April 2003, the company Fast Forward Ltd obtained a court judgement against the cathedral for

£100,000 but found it could not enforce its judgement, nor make any other part of the Church of England pay.

Leaving office

A problem for all church officers is the officer who continues past his 'sell-by date'. Many treasurers can be retired people who have the time, skill and commitment to do an excellent job. Sadly, as some people age, their abilities wane without their realizing it. An excellent treasurer may gradually lose competence as the years pass. This creates a dilemma for the church, which reasonably wishes neither to sack a long-standing loyal servant nor to see its accounts descend into chaos.

There can be no fixed **age limits**, as some treasurers can be competent at eighty while others are incompetent at forty. We recommend the **driving licence model**. When you are seventy, you offer to resign in a manner which makes it easy for the church to accept. This should not be an 'I'll go if you want me to' offer which a church may feel awkward about accepting. If the church asks you to remain, make similar offers at least once every three years thereafter.

Knowing when to **retire** is a matter of discernment; doing so is a matter of grace. You should always retire when still able to continue. A treasurer should never cling to office just to maintain status or to reach a landmark anniversary in post. Give plenty of notice when you wish to retire, make clear that you *will* retire and are not just saying you will, and be ready to afford all assistance to your successor. Have the grace to know when your work is done.

A church must never allow a treasurer (or any other officer) to continue in post when no longer competent to do so. It may be pastorally difficult to ease someone out, but the task must not be shirked. The sensitivities of one individual must never obstruct the mission of the church. Sometimes the task may be done in two stages: suggesting to the individual that it is 'time to move on', and then discussing how and when this will happen. The outgoing treasurer may be appointed assistant treasurer or consultant treasurer, for example. This can help avoid the sense of being thrown on the scrap heap.

If a treasurer proves resistant to standing down, the church authorities should formally request that he resign, and say why. It is always appropriate to be as kind as possible, but not to the extent of being dishonest. If kindness and honesty become incompatible, honesty must prevail. If really necessary, the church authorities must dismiss the treasurer. This may create a pastoral problem, but that should be addressed as a separate issue. However difficult and unpleasant this may be at the time, it is almost certainly the best solution in the long term.

Be reluctant to resign just because you have had problems with the minister or another church officer, or have had a difficult time at the church council or annual meeting. Always look at the underlying causes rather than the personalities. Isolated incidents should be seen as just that. Only if arguments and problems keep happening is it usually necessary to look at the underlying relationships.

If you do think the church authorities are losing trust in you, ask them openly. Be gracious enough to accept that you may no longer be the right person for the job. If the church authorities clearly have lost trust in you, you must resign.

Once you have ceased to be treasurer, never criticize your successor and avoid all comment on how the church finances are managed. It is reasonable still to be interested in the accounts. It is best not to discuss the accounts at all within the church other than with your successor. It is also reasonable for you to be available to your successor for at least a year in answering questions and providing help. But otherwise, let your successor get on with the job.

Guidance on financial ministry

Guidance on debt and other aspects of financial ministry may be obtained from Crown Financial Ministries at http://www.crownuk.org/.

Accounting Terms

This list gives accounting terms most likely to be encountered by church treasurers. The definitions are explanations to help the treasurer to understand what the term means, rather than being a strict legal definition.

account	Category of income or expenditure.
account activity	Term used on bank statements to summarize transactions.
account maintenance	Bank charge, usually made each month, for providing a bank account. Transaction charges are in addition.
account payee	Words added to a crossing on a cheque to indicate that the cheque may only be paid into a bank account in the name of the payee; the cheque cannot be negotiated. This is now standard on almost all cheques.
accountant	Person who is qualified or experienced in accountancy.
accounting basis	The bases which the church has adopted to prepare its accounts, such as the periods over which fixed assets are depreciated.
accounting date	Date to which accounts are made up.
accounting period	Period, usually of one year, for which financial statements are prepared.
accounting principles	Basic principles with which it is assumed all accounts comply unless otherwise stated.

accounting standard	Statement on how accounts must be prepared. These standards are now issued by the Accounting Standards Board.
Accounting Standards Board	Body which issues accounting standards.
accrual	Adjustment in the accounts to reflect liabilities which have been incurred but not yet paid.
accruals basis	Basis of preparing accounts where income and expenditure is adjusted to reflect amounts owing and due for a defined period. This basis is compulsory for churches above a certain size, and optional below that size.
accruals concept	Accounting principle that income and expenditure must be matched in the same accounting period.
Act of God	Natural event for which no human person is responsible, such as lightning. Acts of God are insurable.
ademption	When a legacy fails because the testator did not own the asset at death.
administration	(1) Arrangement whereby an insolvent company has temporary new management. (2) General term for running an organization; listed among the gifts of the Holy Spirit.
administrator	(1) Anyone whose work is general administration. (2) Person who administers the estate of someone who died without leaving a valid will.
administratrix	Female administrator of an intestate estate.
adoption	Process by which members accept the annual report.
advance	Money provided to a trusted person to allow that person to

incur expenditure on behalf of the organization.

advancement of religion   Basis on which churches derive charitable status. Under the Charities Act 2006, the charity must also demonstrate public benefit.

agency   When a person is allowed to act on behalf of someone else. An employee is an agent of the employer.

alms box   Box used to collect funds for charitable purposes.

analysis   Process of apportioning income and expenditure into categories.

annual budget   Budget for a year, usually determined by adjusting figures for previous year.

annual percentage rate   Standard method of expressing interest rates to make them comparable.

annual report   Accounts and other financial information which must be provided to the members each year.

APB   Auditing Practices Board.

appeal commissioners   People who hear appeals against tax assessments.

appreciation   When an asset gains value, as often happens for land.

approval   Process by which the trustees or equivalent body make the treasurer's report their own.

APR   Annual percentage rate. A standard method of expressing interest rates to make them comparable.

arrangement fee   Charge made by a bank or other financial organization for providing you with a service.

asset   Money, something that becomes money, or something worth money.

assign   Any arrangement whereby a benefit is transferred to another person.

ATM   Automated teller machine; cash machine or 'hole in the wall' from

	which cash may be extracted using a debit card.
audit	Investigation into accounts.
audit trail	Ability to trace transactions from source documents to final accounts, and back again.
Auditing Practices Board	Body which issues UK auditing standards.
authorized official	Church officer who operates Gift Aid.
authorized overdraft	Overdraft which the bank agreed in advance.
averaging clause	Provision in most insurance policies that all assets must be insured, and compensation is reduced if a claim is made when there is not full insurance.
BACS	System for making direct payments from a bank account.
balance	Amount of money after transactions have been allowed for.
balance sheet	Summary of the assets and liabilities of an organization at a particular date, indicating the organization's worth.
bank account	Account where a bank holds the funds of the church.
bank charges	Amounts a bank charges its customers for services.
bank holiday	Day when a bank is allowed to close. It is widely also used as a day's paid holiday.
bank loan	Money lent to you by a bank, usually for a fixed period.
bank reconciliation	Document produced to check accounting records against the bank statement.
bank statement	Document provided by bank showing transactions for a period, usually one calendar month.

bankruptcy	When an individual has been legally declared insolvent. The individual must give up most assets and pay what can be paid. The bankrupt is under restrictions until discharged.
Baptist Trust	Model trust available for Baptist churches.
base rate	Rate set by the Bank of England on which most interest rates are based.
basic rate taxpayer	Someone who pays tax at rates only up to 20%.
basket of goods	Representative selection of consumer goods used to calculate inflation.
bazaar	Same as fete.
beneficiary	Person who receives the benefit of a trust.
bill	Invoice (though the word has other meanings).
bill of exchange	Document authorizing payment. A cheque is a form of bill of exchange.
blank cheque	Cheque signed with the amount not entered; a practice which is expressly forbidden.
blessing	Process similar to dedicating an asset, with the same legal and financial consequences (usually none).
bold figure	Figure set in bold type in annual report to draw attention.
book-keeping	That part of the accounting process which involves recording transactions.
books of prime entry	Books or equivalent in which all financial transactions are first recorded.
bought ledger	Another name for purchase ledger.
bouncing (cheque)	Colloquial term for dishonouring.
brackets	Convention that a number has the opposite meaning, so (4) represents −4 rather than +4.
break point	Figure at which point a body must comply with a set of regulations.

Churches have break points of
£100,000 and £250,000.

brought forward   Sub-total from a previous page.

budget   Management decision of what income
and expenditure should be achieved
in a future period.

budget holder   Person who is allowed to spend
church money as allowed in a budget
and who must account for that
spending.

buffer   Amount kept in a bank account in
addition to normal balance to ensure
the account does not accidentally
become overdrawn.

building works insurance   Insurance for building works which
the customer is obliged to provide
under the building contract.

business activity   Commercial activity. If sufficiently
large, the organization must register
for VAT.

calendar year   Period from 1 January to 31
December, used to distinguish a year
from financial year or tax year.

capital   Sum of money distinguished from
revenue or interest. (The word
has many different meanings in
accounting.)

capital endowment   Fund where only the interest may be
spent; the usual form of endowment
fund.

carried forward   Sub-total of a page to be taken to
start of next page.

cash   Money in readily spendable form.

cash book   Book of prime entry for recording
cash transactions.

certified accountant   Member of Association of Chartered
Certified Accountants, now known as
chartered certified accountant.

CHAPS   System for making electronic
payments from a bank account.

charge card	Payment card which allows you to spend money, provided you repay the whole amount within a defined period.
charitable expenditure	Figure in SOFA disclosing how much the church has given to other charitable bodies.
charitable incorporated organization	Legal form currently being proposed for charities.
Charity Commissioners	Body responsible for overseeing charities in England and Wales. Similar bodies are proposed for Scotland and Northern Ireland.
chartered accountant	Member of an accountancy body which has a royal charter.
cheque	Document authorizing the bank to make a payment from an account for a stated amount; a form of bill of exchange.
chip and pin	Arrangement where payment card is authorized by entering a PIN number rather than by signature.
choir children	Children who sing in the church choir, whether paid or not. The law specifically excludes choir children from being regarded as employees of the church.
clearing	Process of making payment from a bank account.
closing the books	Point when the treasurer accepts no further transactions for an accounting period.
codicil	Amendment to a will.
commonhold	Leasehold ownership of land combined with membership of a body which collectively owns common parts, such as corridors and stairs.
Companies House	Where companies must file an annual report and submit their annual accounts.

company voluntary arrangement	Arrangement by an insolvency company which provides a measure of protection against insolvency proceedings.
comparative figure	Figure in annual report giving the equivalent amount for the previous accounting period.
compound interest	Interest calculated by reference to the initial capital plus subsequent amounts of interest.
concept	General term for the principles and similar on which accounting is based.
confidentiality	Duty to keep information secret.
consecration	Legal process of setting aside an asset for sacred use. This usually makes the asset a heritage asset and excludes it from the accounts.
consequential loss	Loss which arises from another loss, such as a loss of income arising from a loss of building. It is possible to insure against consequential loss.
consideration	A benefit provided or a detriment suffered in return for a consideration from the other party. This creates a contract.
consistency concept	Accounting principle that the same accounting policies are used each year unless there is a good reason to change and that is stated in the accounts.
construction industry tax scheme	Tax deduction scheme which must be operated by someone who engages self-employed builders in certain circumstances.
constructive dismissal	When an employee resigns because it is unreasonable to continue working. This is treated as a dismissal.
constructive trust	Trust created by a court.
consumption	Spending money or otherwise using up the value of a current asset.

contingency	Asset or liability which cannot be valued because of a future event. Examples include insurance claims and legal settlements.
contingent work	Provision in a building contract which allows building work to be charged if certain conditions are encountered.
contra	An entry made to reverse another entry, usually when a mistake was made on the first entry.
contract	Legally enforceable agreement between two or more people where each provides a benefit to the other.
contract of employment	Written agreement of terms of employment which the employer must provide within two months of the employment starting.
contractor	Someone other than an employee whom you engage directly to work for you.
corporation sole	The legal person represented by the office rather than the office-holder. So 'the Bishop of Durham' means whoever occupies that office at that time.
cost of generating funds	Figure in SOFA for expenses of generating income, such as cost of stewardship campaign and fund-raising expenses.
countermand	Process of stopping a cheque.
covenant	Legal obligation imposed on land.
CPI	Consumer Price Index, the official measure of inflation since December 2003.
cr	Abbreviation for 'credit'.
credit	Sum deducted from an account. A credit balance represents a liability, income, reduction of asset value or a profit.
credit card	Payment card allowing you to spend

	up to a credit limit and to make payments in instalments if you wish.
credit limit	Maximum amount a financial organization will allow you to incur, such as on a credit card.
creditor	Person to whom you owe money.
cross-casting	Process of analysis in a cash book.
crossing	Two parallel lines drawn or printed on a cheque to restrict how the cheque may be paid. Almost all cheques are now crossed.
current account	Bank account for day-to-day expenditure, usually where a cheque book is provided.
current asset	Cash, debtors and any other asset which is expected to be consumed within the next 12 months.
current cost accounting	Form of inflation accounting abandoned in 1985.
current liability	Liability which must be met within the next 12 months.
current purchase power	Form of inflation accounting which was abandoned before being adopted.
Customs and Excise	Body which collected indirect taxes and performed other duties until merged into HMRC.
day book	Book of prime entry for recording non-cash transactions, such as invoices issued or received.
debit	Sum added to an account. A debit balance represents an asset, expense, reduction of liability or a loss.
debit card	Payment card which allows money to be paid from a bank account.
debt advice agency	Body which gives advice to individuals with debt problems.
debt forgiveness	Voluntarily releasing a person, business or country from a debt.
debtor	Person who owes you money.

dedication	Process of recognizing an asset as for sacred use but which does not change the asset's legal status. Dedicated assets do not usually become heritage assets and must therefore be included in the accounts.
deed of covenant	Legal arrangement for assigning income. For donations, it has now been replaced by Gift Aid.
deficit	Excess of expenditure over income.
deflation	Rate at which prices decrease.
delivery note	Document sent with goods to indicate what should be in the package. It is not an accounting document.
demonstrative legacy	Form of general legacy.
deposit account	Bank account where excess funds are held to earn interest.
depreciation	Cost of consuming a fixed asset.
depreciation threshold	An asset value below which a fixed asset is not depreciated as the depreciation is immaterial.
designated fund	Unrestricted fund which the organization has set aside for a particular purpose.
designated religious body	Term used in Scotland for a church which is excused some compliance provisions for charities.
devise	Gift of land and buildings in a will.
devisee	Someone who receives a devise.
difference finding	Procedure to find a mistake in cross-casting.
diocese	Central authority of Anglican or Roman Catholic Church, roughly corresponding in size to a county.
direct debit	Strictly controlled arrangement whereby an approved supplier may withdraw payments from your bank account for varying amounts.
direct tax	Tax on earnings, such as income tax, corporation tax and capital gains tax.

dirty money	Money obtained from improper source, such as crime.
disclaimer	Refusal to accept a legacy or other gift.
discrepancy	Situation where financial reality does not accord with the financial records.
discretionary fund	Fund which may be used for a payment approved by a fund holder. Such a fund is often held by a church minister to meet sensitive expenditure such as to relieve poverty of a church member.
discretionary trust	Special trust where trustees must exercise judgement.
discrimination	In employment law, the imposition of a bar or restriction on a person because of some characteristic. Some forms of discrimination are illegal.
dishonour (cheque)	When a bank refuses to pay a cheque for which funds are not available in the bank account.
dismissal	Termination of employment by the employer.
district church council	In the Church of England, a body with some oversight function for part of a parish but which is not itself a legal entity.
double-entry book-keeping	System of book-keeping where every transaction is recorded by debits and credits of equal amounts.
double underline	Indication that the number double underlined is a total.
dr	Abbreviation for 'debit'.
driving licence model	Arrangement whereby a church officer offers to retire on reaching 70 and at least once every three years thereafter to ensure that the officer does not continue past 'sell-by date'.
e-banking	Internet banking or similar computer-based banking.

educational trust	Trust created by education law applying to funds when land from a church school has been sold.
employee	Someone who is under the control of an employer. Significant tax, national insurance and pension liabilities follow from this status. There are many doubtful areas in church life.
employers' liability insurance	Insurance cover which legally every employer must have to protect its employees.
endowment fund	Fund where, generally, only the interest may be spent.
entry	Details of a transaction entered into the financial records.
equal pay	Legal requirement that a woman must be paid the same rate as a man doing the same or equivalent work.
equity release	Scheme to release capital from property.
estate	The value of property left by someone who has died (among other definitions).
estimate	(1) A statement of how much a contractor or supplier expects to charge for goods or services. An estimate is not legally binding on the contractor or supplier. (2) A figure in the accounts when the exact figure is not known. The accounts must say that an estimate has been used.
ex gratia payment	Payment which a church is not legally obliged to pay but does so from a sense of moral obligation. Such payments must be disclosed in the annual report.
excepted charity	Church which need not submit accounts to the Charity Commissioners.
excess	In insurance, the amount of a loss

you bear yourself. The insurance company pays only for the loss above the amount of the excess.

exclusion clause — Provision in an insurance policy stating when the insurance company will not pay against a claim.

executor — Person who administers the estate of someone who has died and made a valid will.

executrix — Female executor.

expendable endowment — Rare form of endowment where the capital may be spent as well as the interest.

expenditure — Money spent or owed by an organization.

exposure draft — Draft of an accounting standard.

extinguishment — Ending of a debt other than by payment.

extra-statutory concession — Provision made by tax authority to relax a tax law in a narrow area.

fete — Fund-raising activity comprising stalls and sideshows. This is a trading activity in the church accounts. A fete requires compliance with a host of legal requirements.

fidelity insurance — Insurance against misappropriation of funds by a church officer.

Finance Act — Annual act of parliament amending tax law.

financial planning — Process of making arrangements for efficient future of funds to cover foreseeable eventualities, to minimize outgoings and to maximize income.

Financial Reporting Exposure Draft — Draft of a Financial Reporting Standard.

Financial Reporting Standard — A UK accounting standard issued by the Accounting Standards Board.

financial statement — A report of financial activity, such as statement of financial activities or summary of assets and liabilities.

financial year	The year for which financial statements are prepared, which may not be the same as the calendar year. The term 'accounting period' is now preferred.
fixed asset	Buildings, furniture and other assets which are not expected to be consumed within the next twelve months.
fixed-price contract	A contract where the exact price is stated at the outset.
fixed rate	Rate (usually of interest) which does not change for a defined period.
flexible budget	Budget which allows for variations depending on circumstances.
float system	System where petty cash is periodically topped up with sufficient funds.
forced realization	When it is assumed that the organization will not continue in being, usually because it is insolvent, and is not a 'going concern'. Forced realization usually means that assets have a much-reduced value.
forecast	Expectation of what will happen in a current or future accounting period.
forgery	Any document which is not what it seems. Forgery can be a criminal offence.
FRED	Financial Reporting Exposure Draft.
freehold	Ownership of land and all that is on it, under it and over it.
freewill offering	Voluntary gift from church member.
friends group	Body set up to help another body but which is legally independent of that other body.
FRS	Financial Reporting Standard.
functional fixed asset	Item of tangible property which is intended to further the mission of the church.
fund	Amount of money available to an organization and categorized according to how it may be spent.

fund raising	Any activity primarily conducted to generate income.
FWO	Freewill offering.
GAAP	Generally accepted accounting principles.
gaming	Game of chance played for winnings, such as bingo and whist drives. Above a certain limit, a licence is needed.
GAYE	Give as you earn.
gearing	Relationship whereby a small increase in one figure can lead to a large increase in another.
general crossing	Crossing on a cheque which is not a special crossing. Such a cheque must be paid into a bank account and cannot be cashed by the holder.
general fund	The unrestricted funds of an organization.
general legacy	Legacy of identifiable but not specified property.
generally accepted accounting principles	Collective term for all relevant accounting standards.
Gift Aid	Scheme which allows tax to be reclaimed on donations.
gift day	Day set aside for church members to make gifts to the church, usually in addition to their regular giving and for a specific purpose.
GIGO	Garbage in garbage out – a colloquialism which means the quality of computer output depends on quality of input.
Give as you earn	Another name for payroll giving.
going concern	The accounting principle which assumes that the entity will continue in being for the foreseeable future. The opposite is forced realization.
good faith	When someone acts from a proper motive even if the decision

	subsequently proves to be unwise. This concept is relevant in such areas as trustee insurance.
grant	Donation made to or received by a church, usually as a single payment for a specific object.
grey software	Illegally copied software.
gross pay	Amount an employee earns before any deductions are made.
harassment	Two or more actions designed to annoy or distress a person. It can be a criminal offence.
heritage asset	Fixed asset which cannot be disposed of without special permission and which is excluded from the accounts.
HICP	Harmonized Index of Consumer Prices; the full name for CPI, a measure of inflation now used in all European Union countries.
higher rate taxpayer	Someone who pays income tax at rates up to 40%.
historic and inalienable assets	Term used before March 2005 for heritage assets.
historic cost convention	Widely used accounting basis which ignores the fact that money has lost value during the accounting period.
historic resources	Funds derived from past giving.
HM Revenue and Customs	The UK tax authority formed on 18 April 2005 from Inland Revenue and Customs and Excise.
HMRC	HM Revenue and Customs.
holding trustees	Trustees who hold the church building and other assets for benefit of members, usually distinguished from managing trustees.
holiday	When an employee is allowed to be absent for rest. The law requires at least 5.6 weeks' paid holiday.
hostage customer	Bank customer who cannot clear an overdraft and is therefore at the

	mercy of the bank when it imposes interest and charges.
house-to-house collection	Raising funds by going from house to house, such as when carol singing. A licence from the police is needed.
human resources	The discipline of managing people effectively. It involves such areas as motivation and leadership.
hygiene factor	A factor which does not improve an employee's productivity but whose absence reduces productivity. The amount of pay is a hygiene factor.
hyperinflation	When inflation exceeds 100% over three years. Special accounting provisions then apply.
IAS	International Accounting Standard.
identification number	Code giving access to a bank account on the Internet.
IFRS	International Financial Reporting Standard.
illiquidity	Inability to convert an asset to cash.
immaterial	Not material; refers to a figure which is so small that it does not affect the picture painted by the accounts.
imprest system	System where petty cash is topped up with the value of vouchers so that the total of cash plus vouchers is always the same figure.
income	Money received or receivable by an organization.
income and expenditure account	Form once used to record income and expenditure, now replaced by receipts and payments account.
income in kind	Donations other than in cash.
income tax	Tax on a person's earnings. If the church is the employer, the church must deduct income tax under PAYE.
incoming resources	Figure in SOFA for all forms of income.

incumbent and churchwardens trust	Trust held for the benefit of a Church of England church. It is either a special trust or must be registered as a charity.
independent examination	Review of accounts which falls short of a full audit.
indirect tax	Tax on spending, such as value added tax, excise duty and customs duties.
individual voluntary arrangement	Arrangement by an insolvent person which provides a measure of protection against bankruptcy.
inflation	Rate at which prices increase.
inflation accounting	System designed to allow for the fact that money has lost value during the accounting period. No system of inflation accounting is currently recognized in the UK.
inheritance tax	Tax paid on the estate of someone who has died.
Inland Revenue	Body charged with collecting direct taxes and other duties before being merged into HMRC.
insolvency	Financial state of owing more than you own. In itself it imposes no legal restrictions, but can be a basis for restrictions.
insurance	Arrangement where the church pays a premium so that it is compensated if it suffers a predetermined loss.
intangible asset	Asset which has no physical form, such as copyright, patent or goodwill.
intangible income	Benefit donated to the church other than cash or a tangible asset, such as free use of office space or free printing.
interest	Sum paid to borrow money (interest payable), or received for lending or depositing money (interest receivable).
international accounting standard	Accounting standard intended to be applied internationally, issued by the

International Accounting Standards Board.

Internet banking   Banking where transactions are effected on the Internet.

intestate   A person who has no valid will to dispose of property on death.

investment   An asset held for the primary purpose of generating income.

invoice   Document which confirms that a supplier has supplied goods or services.

IOU   Personal loan authorized by the borrower; not recommended.

JCT contract   Contract used for most forms of building project.

journal   Book recording debits and credits in double-entry book-keeping.

key area   One of twelve objects which a body must meet to be given charitable status.

land   Fixed asset which is uniquely never depreciated. Its value must be separated from that of any buildings on it.

lay rector   Landowner who is liable to repair the chancel of a Church of England building.

lease   Right to occupy or possess property for a period with some legal rights but not ownership.

leasehold   Ownership of land to a stated date.

ledger   Record of transactions outside the double-entry book-keeping system but needed for other purposes, such as a sales ledger to identify who owes you money.

legacy   Gift of cash or other personal property in a will.

legal entity	A legal person; the body to whom the funds belong.
legal expenses insurance	Insurance against legal expenses either in bringing or defending a claim whether or not the matter goes to court.
legal tender	Notes and coins accepted as money in England and Wales.
legatee	Someone who receives a legacy.
lending	Giving money to someone with the expectation of having the money returned.
letter of administration	Authority given to an administrator to deal with the estate of someone who died without leaving a valid will.
liability	An obligation to pay money.
licence	Right to occupy property without acquiring any ownership.
liquidation	Ending of a company when its assets are sold to pay debts.
liquidity	Ease with which an asset may be turned into cash. Cash is the most liquid asset, and fixed assets the least liquid.
local ecumenical project	A church used by the Church of England and at least one other denomination under a formal agreement.
long-term liability	Liability which need not be met for more than twelve months.
loss	Reduction in wealth generated by the activities of a commercial entity.
lottery	Distribution of prizes between those who pay on a basis which does not require any skill by the payers. A lottery may need a licence.
magnetic ink	Used on cheques, allowing data to be read automatically.
managing trustees	Trustees who manage the church on

	a day-to-day basis, unlike holding trustees.
mandate	Instructions to the bank on who may sign cheques.
Maslow's hierarchy	The five levels of need which must be met in order for staff to be motivated.
matching concept	Another name for accruals concept.
material acquisition	The purchase of an item whose amount is so substantial that it significantly reduces the liquid funds. Such an acquisition must be disclosed in the annual report.
materiality	Accounting principle that the accounts should not be cluttered with detail about amounts which are so small that they do not affect the picture painted by the accounts.
memorandum account	Any form of financial record outside double-entry book-keeping. A ledger is a memorandum account.
ministerial trust	Special trust which requires only normal business skills.
monetarism	Accounting principle that the accounts only reflect items to which a value in money terms may be ascribed.
money laundering	Any process which is designed to take dirty money (such as from crime) and make it look clean. It is a crime not to report suspicion of money laundering.
mortgage	Loan secured on property.
mortgagee	Person who lends money in a mortgage.
mortgagor	Person who borrows money in a mortgage.
motivation	Matching an employee's objectives to the employer's to maximize productivity.
motivator	Those factors which improve an employee's productivity.

narrative report	That part of the annual report which does not comprise figures.
national insurance	A compulsory deduction from pay, now regarded as a tax, which funds social security payments.
national minimum wage	The minimum hourly rate you must pay an employee.
negotiation	In banking, a procedure whereby a payee may assign a cheque to someone else. This is done by writing instructions and signing on back. An 'account payee' cheque cannot be negotiated.
net book value	Value of a fixed asset at any time, usually calculated as cost minus depreciation.
net pay	Amount that an employee earns after statutory deductions are made.
netting off	Process where expenditure is deducted from matching income, such as showing only the profit from magazine sales rather than separate figures for magazine sales and magazine costs. In general, figures should not be netted off.
nominal ledger	Where debit and credit balances are recorded from books of prime entry, and from where the trial balance is extracted.
non-monetary item	Item which is not money but has a value.
notes to the accounts	Additional explanation and analysis provided with the financial statements and forming part of the annual accounts.
notice period	The length of time an employer or employee must give the other when intending to end an employment. There are statutory minimum notice periods.

OCRA	Stylized form of text used on cheques allowing them to be optically read.
open cheque	Cheque which has no crossing and which may therefore be cashed by the holder. Open cheques are now very rare.
outgoing resources	Figure in SOFA for all forms of expenditure and liability.
overdraft	Balance on a bank account when the customer has made payments for which funds are not available.
ownership	Having legal title to goods rather than just physical custody. Ownership is a package of legal rights.
parent body	Body to which another body is accountable.
parochial church council	A legal entity of the Church of England.
parochial trust	Trust which administers local welfare trusts established before 1948.
part-timer	Someone working less than a full working week. The law requires part-timers to be treated as fairly as full-timers.
password	Secret combination of numbers and letters giving access to a computer file.
Pay As You Earn	System of deducting income tax and national insurance at source which must be used by all employers.
payee	Someone to whom a payment is made.
payment card	Any form of plastic card which may be used in a financial transaction. Main types are credit card, charge card and debit card.
payroll	The records for paying employees. The payroll is a book of prime entry.
payroll giving	Method of giving tax relief on donations made from payroll.

payslip	Itemized statement which must be legally provided every time an employee is paid.
pecuniary legacy	Legacy of cash.
Performing Rights Society	Body which issues licences allowing recorded music to be played at a public function such as a church fete.
peril	Defined risk against which you take out insurance.
permanent endowment	Another name for a capital endowment fund.
perpetuity	Legal rule which restricts how far an inheritance can be tied up by a testator.
personal accident insurance	Insurance cover for church volunteers.
personal property	Property other than land and buildings.
personalty	Property other than land and buildings.
petty cash	Ready cash kept on the premises for small items of expenditure.
PIN number	Four-digit personal identification number which allows you to authorize a transaction made by payment card.
pledged giving	System by which church members promise to make regular contributions.
political discrimination	Discrimination because of a person's political views. It is illegal in Northern Ireland, but not in Great Britain.
possession	Having physical custody even though you may not own the goods.
pre-preferential debt	Expenses of an insolvency, which are paid before all other debts.
predeceasing	Dying before you inherit.
preferential debt	Debt which ranks before other debts other than pre-preferential debts.
prepayment	Amount paid in advance for a

	service, such as for rent or a telephone line.
priority debt	Debt which must be paid before other debts.
private trust	Trust benefiting one person or small group.
probate	Right of executor to administer estate of deceased person.
profit	Wealth generated by the activities of a commercial entity.
profit and loss	Financial statement indicating how much profit or loss has been made by a commercial entity over a period.
project supervisor	Person entrusted with oversight of a major church project, such as major building or repair work.
property	Anything which is capable of being owned.
prosperity inflation	Excess by which inflation is exceeded by wage inflation, traditionally about two percentage points.
provision	Sum set aside to meet a future liability.
prudence concept	Accounting principle that accounts should err on the side of understating the financial position rather than overstating it.
public benefit	Criterion for giving charitable status under the Charities Act 2006.
public collection	Raising funds from a public place other than by going from house to house, such as carol singing in a town centre. A local authority licence is needed.
public liability insurance	Insurance cover to protect you against claims which may be made by members of the public.
public trust	Trust benefiting the general public or a large part of it.
publication	Process of making the annual report known to members. There are various

	rules about method and time limits for publication.
purchase ledger	Record of how much you owe your suppliers.
qualified report	Report by auditor or examiner which discloses a concern or which gives information not included in the accounts.
quotation	A statement of how much a contractor or supplier will charge for providing goods or a service. A quotation is legally binding for a stated period, unlike an estimate.
racial discrimination	Discrimination against a person on the grounds of their colour, race or ethnic origin. It is generally illegal.
real property	Land and buildings.
realization	Process for turning assets into cash, particularly in insolvency.
realty	Land and buildings.
receipts and payments	Basis of preparing accounts where the accounts show only actual receipts and payments made during the period regardless of the period to which they relate. The alternative basis is accruals basis which is compulsory when a church's finances exceed defined limits.
receipts and payments account	Record of income and expenditure for a church which need not prepare accruals accounts.
receivership	When an insolvent company has its management replaced and possibly parts of the business sold.
recipient	Someone who receives a payment.
recognition	Point at which income or expenditure is sufficiently certain to be included in the accounts.

redundancy	Dismissal of an employee because their work is no longer needed. There are legal consequences.
redundancy pay	Amount an employer is required to pay an employee who has been made redundant.
registered auditor	Accountant who is allowed to audit accounts.
registration limit	Figure of annual turnover when an organization must register for VAT.
related party transaction	Financial transaction between the church and a member of its ruling body. Such transactions must be disclosed in the annual report.
religious discrimination	Discrimination against a person because of their religion. A church may discriminate on these grounds only for areas where religious belief is related to the work.
remittance advice	Document which gives details of income.
replacement cheque	Cheque issued to replace one which was stopped, dishonoured or went stale.
residuary legacy	Legacy of whatever is left when all other legacies have been paid.
restricted fund	Fund which legally may only be used for a limited purpose.
resulting trust	Trust which arises from the conduct of the parties.
RIBA	Royal Institute of British Architects. Their contracts are widely used for building projects.
risk assessment	Formal process of determining risks faced by the church according to likelihood and impact. This is obligatory in larger churches.
royal charter	Method by which a charity may come into existence.
RPA	Receipts and payments account.

RPI	Retail Prices Index; the official measure of inflation until December 2003, when replaced by CPI.
rule of 72	Mathematical observation that if you divide 72 by an interest rate, the answer is the approximate number of years it takes for your money to double using compound interest at that rate.
running total	Sum of figures to which further figures will be added.
sales ledger	Record of how much your customers owe you.
SAS	Statement of Auditing Standard.
scam	Fraud perpetrated by pretence.
Schedule B	Form which must be completed by Methodist treasurers.
secured creditor	Person to whom money is owed under a secured loan.
secured loan	Money which has been lent on the basis that defined property may be seized if the loan is not repaid.
security	Provisions taken to reduce risks, and which can therefore lead to a reduction in insurance premium.
self-employed	Someone who works for you but not under such control as to make them an employee. Great care must be exercised in ensuring that a person is legally within the scope of self-employment to avoid tax liabilities.
sell-by date	Colloquial term for when an officer has reached the end of their ability to continue doing their job.
separate valuation concept	Accounting principle that assets and liabilities must be separately disclosed and not netted off.
settlor	Person who provides property in a trust.
sexual discrimination	Discrimination against a person on

the grounds of their sex, marital
status or pregnancy. It is generally
illegal.

sexual orientation Whether a person (male or female)
is heterosexual or homosexual. A
church may discriminate on grounds
of sexual orientation if that is its
stated and consistent policy.

signatory Person authorized to sign documents
for an organization.

signature Stylized form of a person writing
his or her name to indicate that that
person authorizes the document.

simple interest Interest calculated by reference to the
initial capital only.

simple trust Trust created simply by passing
property to trustee.

small lottery Tombola, raffle and similar which
does not need a licence provided
relevant conditions are met.

small print Terms and conditions which apply to
a contract and which must always be
read before agreeing the contract.

small trades Incidental trading. Below a threshold
it avoids tax.

small works contract Contract for building work of less
than £150,000.

society lottery Lottery other than a small lottery
for which a local authority licence is
needed.

SOFA Statement of Financial Activities.

software Programs and similar which run
computers.

SORP Statement of Recommended Practice;
a statement which bodies in particular
areas are expected to follow when
preparing accounts. Churches should
follow the charities SORP.

special crossing Crossing on a cheque with a place
or name of bank indicated. Such a

	cheque may only be cashed at that place or bank. Special crossings are now rare.
special trust (1)	Funds administered on behalf of a church or charity for a special purpose.
special trust (2)	Simple trust where the trustee has duties to perform.
specific legacy	When a specific item of property is left to someone in a will.
sponsorship	A commercial arrangement whereby a business provides funds in return for receiving a benefit from the church. The word is also used for agreeing to pay a sum to someone undertaking an activity to raise funds, such as agreeing to pay someone £10 if they run a marathon.
squirrelling	Colloquial term for the non-recommended practice of creating designated funds solely to reduce the stated surplus.
SSAP	Statement of Standard Accounting Practice.
stale cheque	Cheque which the payee has not paid into their account and where the time limit for doing so (usually six months) has expired.
stamp duty land tax	Tax payable on property transactions.
standing order	Arrangement whereby a fixed amount is paid at regular intervals, such as for pledged giving by church members.
statement	Document which summarizes invoices owing, usually supplied at the end of each month.
statement of assets and liabilities	Statement of assets and liabilities of a church which prepares a receipts and payments account.
Statement of Auditing Standard UK	Auditing standard issued by Auditing Practices Board.

statement of financial activities	Record of income and expenditure produced by a church using the accruals basis.
statement of standard accounting practice	UK accounting standard issued between 1971 and 1990.
statutory adoption pay	Amount an employer is required to pay to a man or woman who adopts a child.
statutory instrument	Secondary legislation approved by a government minister under powers contained in an Act of Parliament.
statutory maternity pay	Amount an employer is required to pay a woman who is absent because of pregnancy and childbirth.
statutory paternity pay	Amount an employer is required to pay to a man whose wife gives birth, or to a man or woman whose partner adopts a child.
statutory sick pay	Amount an employer is required to pay an employee who is off work because of sickness or injury.
statutory trust	Trust created by an Act of Parliament.
stewardship	Responsible attitude of church members to their possessions, money and talents. This includes the members being generous in giving and the trustees being accountable to the members.
stopped cheque	Cheque you have issued but where you subsequently tell the bank not to pay it, usually because the cheque has been lost or misappropriated.
straight line method	Method of depreciating a fixed asset in equal instalments over its economic life.
subcontractor	Someone a contractor engages to do some of the work for which you have engaged the contractor.
substance over form	Accounting principle that the accounts should reflect the financial

	reality of a situation even when this differs from the legal form.
sub-total	Sum of figures which is itself to be added to other figures.
summary dismissal	Instant dismissal when an employee's conduct is such that the employer cannot reasonably expect the employment to continue during a notice period.
sundry	Income or expenditure which does not fall within any other category.
surplus	Excess of income over expenditure.
SWOT principle	General management principle of identifying strengths, weaknesses, opportunities and threats.
take-home pay	Amount of net pay an employee receives after all deductions have been made.
tangible asset	Asset which has a physical form, such as a building, furniture, chattel or vehicle.
tariff	Any list of prices, such as for bank charges.
tart	Colloquial term for someone who keeps changing banks or other financial suppliers to benefit from special offers.
tax avoidance	Legal act of minimizing tax liability within the law.
tax evasion	Illegal act of suppressing or falsifying tax information.
team	In the Church of England, parishes linked together but which remain separate legal entities and must produce separate accounts.
temporary event notice	Form of licence needed from a local authority to sell alcohol at a church fete.
testacy	When someone has a valid will to dispose of property on death.

testate	A person who has a valid will to dispose of property on death.
testator	Person who has made a will disposing of property on death.
testatrix	Female testator.
testimonial	Gift in cash or otherwise made to reflect appreciation for a person rather than as payment for services. A testimonial is generally exempt from tax and national insurance.
three-fourteenths trust	Educational trust commonly found in the Church of England.
time work	Work paid for according to time spent.
tithe	Traditional offering of one-tenth of one's income to the church.
trading	In the context of church accounts, any activity which involves expenditure to generate income (such as hall letting or magazine sales), even if income generation is not the main purpose of the activity.
transaction	Any activity or accounting adjustment requiring an entry in the financial records.
transaction charge	Charge made by a bank for each transaction, in addition to any account maintenance charge.
travel insurance	Insurance against losses suffered while travelling.
treasurer	Officer responsible for looking after funds in a church or other non-commercial organization.
trial balance	List of debit and credit balances taken from nominal ledger or prime books of account. The final accounts are prepared from the trial balance.
TRIO	The responsibility is ours; slogan of United Reformed Church.
true and fair	Overriding principle which applies to all accounts prepared under the accruals basis.

trust	Arrangement whereby one person holds property for the benefit of another.
trust deed	Document formally establishing a trust.
trust for ecclesiastical purposes	Special trust for a specified purpose (such as maintaining the churchyard) for which special legal provisions apply.
trust for saying masses	Trust established to say masses for the deceased. This is a trust of imperfect obligation unless the mass is public.
trust of imperfect obligation	Trust with no human beneficiary, which a trustee may administer but cannot be compelled to do so.
trustee	Person who holds property in trust for the benefit of another.
trustee insurance	Insurance which protects the trustees (or equivalent) of a church against claims for negligence when the trustees were acting in good faith.
trustees' expenses	Expenses of members of the church's governing body. This figure must be separately disclosed in the annual report.
UITF abstract	Statement from the Urgent Issues Tax Force which has the force of an accounting standard.
unauthorized overdraft	Overdraft which the bank has not agreed in advance but is prepared to allow, usually at a high interest rate and with high bank charges.
unauthorized purchase	When a church member ostensibly buys goods or makes a contract without authority. The treasurer must refer all such cases to the church council before paying for the goods.
uncertainty	Vagueness in expressing a provision of a contract or will so that it cannot be enforced.

uncleared cheque	Cheque that has been issued but not cleared by your bank.
uncleared effects	Payment made into your bank but which has yet to appear on the bank statement.
underline	Indication that the number below is a sub-total.
unfair dismissal	Dismissal of an employee for an improper reason.
unincorporated association	Body formed by individuals where the individuals remain fully liable for the debts of the body.
united benefice	Arrangement of Church of England parishes where each parish remains a separate entity which must prepare its own accounts.
unlawful dismissal	Dismissal of an employee in an improper manner, such as by not giving notice or warnings.
unqualified report	Report by auditor or examiner which discloses no concerns.
unrestricted fund	Fund which may be used for any purpose.
unsecured creditor	Person to whom money is owed under an unsecured loan.
unsecured loan	Loan which is not secured.
Urgent Issues Tax Force	Body which prepares accounting abstracts to deal with narrow accounting issues, usually particularly topical ones.
useful economic life	Period over which a fixed asset is expected to last and over which it is depreciated.
usury	In Old Testament, (generally) the charging of interest on a loan to relieve poverty. Today the word usually means extortionate interest.
valuation	Process of ascribing a monetary value to an item.
value added tax (VAT)	Sales tax on goods and services.

Churches are disadvantaged in that they cannot reclaim VAT as most businesses and other non-commercial bodies can.

variable rate
Rate which varies during a defined period, commonly an interest rate which is linked to the base rate.

void legacy
Legacy which cannot legally be effected.

volunteer
Someone who agrees to work for the church without payment. Such a person must be covered by public accident insurance, and may be paid only genuine expenses.

voucher
Any document which gives details of a financial transaction.

wage inflation
Rate at which wages increase.

will
Legally binding instructions as to what happens to your property when you die.

withering on the vine
Allowing the value of money to reduce over a long period through inflation.

wizard
Program which installs computer software.

zero-based budget
Budget which does not use previous year's figures but where every figure is considered afresh, particularly where expenditure must be wholly justified each year.

Useful Addresses

To contact the author:
Robert Leach
19 Chestnut Avenue, Ewell, Epsom, Surrey KT19 0SY.
Telephone: 020 8224 5695
E-mail: robert.leach627@ntlworld.com
Website: www.robertleach.co.uk

Other contact addresses
The inclusion of an organization or company below should not be taken as a recommendation by the author or publishers. Readers must make their own assessment before entering into any arrangement.

Association of Church Accountants and Treasurers
c/o CDFG, CAN Mezzanine, 49–51 East Road, Old Street, London N1 5AH.
Telephone: 0845 564 2280
E-mail: admin@acat.uk.com
Website: www.acat.uk.com

Ansvar Insurance Company
Ansvar House, St Leonard's Road, Eastbourne, East Sussex BN21 3UR.
Telephone: 01323 737 541
E-mail: ansvar.insurance@ansvar.co.uk
Website: www.ansvar.co.uk

Arts Council of England [grant-making body]
14 Great Peter Street, London SW1P 3NQ.
Telephone: 0845 300 6200 / 6100
Website: www.artscouncil.org.uk

Assemblies of God Inc.
PO Box 7634, Nottingham NG11 6ZY.
Telephone: 0115 921 7272
E-mail: info@aog.org.uk
Website: www.aog.org.uk

Association of Charitable Foundations
Central House, 14 Upper Woburn Place, London WC1H 0AE.
Telephone: 0207 255 4499
E-mail: acf@acf.org.uk
Website: www.acf.org.uk

Association of Charity Independent Examiners
The Gatehouse, White Cross, South Road, Lancaster, LA1 4XQ.
Telephone: 01524 34892
E-mail: info@acie.org.uk
Website: www.acie.org.uk

Association of Charity Officers
Five Ways, 57/59 Hatfield Road, Potters Bar, Hertfordshire, EN6 1HS.
Telephone: 01707 651 777
E-mail: info@aco.uk.net
Website: www.ncvo-vol.org.uk/advice-support/umbrella-bodies-directory/aco

Association of Chartered Certified Accountants
29 Lincoln's Inn Fields, London WC2A 3EE.
Telephone: 0207 059 5000
E-mail: info@accaglobal.com
Website: www2.accaglobal.com/uk

Association of Christian Financial Advisers
PO Box 728, Rickmansworth, WD3 0HT.
Telephone: 07583 349 229
E-mail: acfa@live.co.uk
Website: www.christianfinancialadvisers.org.uk

Baptist Insurance Company plc
Beaufort House, Brunswick Road, Gloucester GL1 1JZ.
Telephone: 01452 334 930
E-mail: enquiries@baptist-ins.com
Website: www.baptist-insurance.co.uk

Baptist Union of Great Britain
Baptist House, PO Box 44, 129 Broadway, Didcot OX11 8RT.
Telephone: 01235 517 700
E-mail: info@baptist.org.uk
Website: www.baptist.org.uk

Baptist Union of Scotland
48 Speirs Wharf, Glasgow, G4 9TH.
Telephone: 0141 423 6169
E-mail: admin@scottishbaptist.org.uk
Website: www.scottishbaptist.org.uk

Baptist Union of Wales
Y Llwyfan, Trinity College, College Road, Carmarthen, SA31 3EQ.
Telephone: 01267 245 660
E-mail: revthmc@mcmanus78.freeserve.co.uk
Website: www.buw.org.uk

CCL Ltd [copyright licences]
Chantry House, 22 Upperton Road, Eastbourne, BN21 1BF.
Telephone: 01323 417 711
E-mail: info@ccli.co.uk
Website: www.ccli.co.uk

CCLA Investment Management Ltd
80 Cheapside, London EC2V 6DZ.
Telephone: 0800 022 3505
E-mail: clientservices@ccla.co.uk
Website: www.ccla.co.uk

Charities Aid Foundation
25 Kings Hill Avenue, Kings Hill, West Malling, Kent ME19 4TA.
Telephone: 03000 123 000
E-mail: enquires@cafonline.org
Website: www.cafonline.org

Charity Commission
PO Box 1227, Liverpool, L69 3UG.
Telephone: 0845 300 0218
E-mail: enquiries@charitycommission.gsi.gov.uk
Website: www.charity-commission.gov.uk

Charity Finance Directors' Group
CAN Mezzanine, 49-51 East Road, London, N1 6AH.
Telephone: 0845 345 3192
E-mail: info@cfdg.org.uk
Website: www.cfdg.org.uk

Charity Giving
PO Box 92, Dereham NR20 4WD.
Telephone: 0845 130 3683
E-mail: contactus@dovetrust.com
Website: www.charitygiving.co.uk

Charity Law Association
Telephone: 01634 373 253.
E-mail: admin@charitylawassociation.org.uk
Website: www.charitylawassociation.org.uk

Charity Tax Group
Church House, Great Smith Street, London, SW1P 3AZ.
Telephone: 0207 222 1265
E-mail: info@ctrg.org.uk
Website: www.ctrg.org.uk

Chartered Institute of Management Accountants (CIMA)
Enquiry Centre, 26 Chapter Street, London, SW1P 4NP.
Telephone: 0208 849 2251
E-mail: callback@cimaglobal.com
Website: www.cimaglobal.com

Chartered Institute of Public Finance and Accountancy (CIPFA)
3 Robert Street, London WC2N 6RL.
Telephone: 0207 543 5600
E-mail: corporate@cipfa.org.uk
Website: www.cipfa.org.uk

Christian Brethren
Abbey Court, Cove, Tiverton EX16 7RT.
Telephone: 01398 331 105

Churchcare
Cathedral and Church Buildings Division, Archbishops' Council, Church House,
Great Smith Street, London SW1P 3AZ.
Telephone: 0207 898 1863
Email:ccb@churchofengland.org
Website: www.churchcare.co.uk

Church Commissioners for England
Church House, Great Smith Street, London, SW1P 3AZ.
Telephone: 0207 898 1000
E-mail: commissioners.enquiry@c-of-e.org.uk
Website: www.churchofengland.org/about-us/structure/
churchcommissioners.aspx

Church in Wales
39 Cathedral Road, Cardiff CF11 9XT.
Telephone: 02920 348 200
E-mail: information@churchinwales.org.uk
Website: www.churchinwales.org.uk

Church of England Archbishops' Council and General Synod
Church House, Great Smith Street, London SW1P 3NZ.
Telephone: 0207 898 1000
Website: www.churchofengland.org/about-us/structure/
archbishopscouncil.aspx

Church of England Pensions Board
29 Great Smith Street, Westminster, London SW1P 3PS.
Telephone: 0207 898 1802
E-mail: pensions@churchofengland.org
Website: www.churchofengland.org/clergy-office-holders/pensions-
and-housing/pensions.aspx

Church of Ireland
Church Avenue, Rathmines, Dublin 6, Republic of Ireland.
Telephone: 00 353 1 4978422
E-mail: enquiries@ireland.anglican.org
Website: www.ireland.anglican.org

Church of Scotland
121 George Street, Edinburgh EH2 4YN.
Telephone: 0131 225 5722
E-mail: webenquiries@cofscotland.org.uk
Website: www.churchofscotland.org.uk

Churches' Child Protection Advisory Service (CCPAS)
PO Box 133, Swanley, Kent BR8 7UQ.
Telephone: 0845 120 4552
E-mail: info@ccpas.co.uk
Website: www.cpas.co.uk

Churches Main Committee
1 Millbank, London SW1P 3JZ.
Telephone: 0207 222 1265
E-mail: cmc@c-of-e.org.uk
Website: www.cmainc.org.uk

Churches Together in England
27 Tavistock Square, London WC1H 9HH.
Telephone: 0207 529 8131
Website@ www.cte.org.uk

Churches Together in Scotland
Inglewood House, Alloa, Clackmananshire, FK10 2HU.
Telephone: 01259 215 964
Website: http://www.acts-scotland.org

Congregational and General Insurance
Currer House, Currer Street, Bradford, West Yorkshire BD1 5BA.
Telephone: 01274 700 700
E-mail: cgi@cgins.co.uk
Website: www.congregational.co.uk

Credit Action
6th Floor, Lynton House, 7-12 Tavistock Square, London, WC1H 9LT.
Telephone: 0207 380 3390
E-mail: office@creditaction.org.uk
Website: www.creditaction.com

Criminal Records Bureau
PO Box 110, Liverpool L3 6ZZ.
Telephone: 0870 909 0811; registration: 0870 909 0822
E-mail: customerservices@crb.gsi.gov.uk
Website: www.homeoffice.gov.uk/agencies-public-bodies/crb/

Customs and Excise – see HM Revenue and Customs.

Data Developments [church accounting software]
Wolverhampton Science Park, Stafford Road, Wolverhampton,
WV10 9RU.
Telephone: 01902 824 044
E-mail: sales@data-developments.co.uk
Website: www.datadevelopments.co.uk

Data Protection – see Information Commissioner

Debt Solutions
Havering Grange, Havering Road, Romford RM1 4HR.
Telephone: 0800 011 2435
E-mail: advice@freefromdebt.org.uk
Website: www.debt-solutions.co.uk

Ecclesiastical Insurance Group
Beaufort House, Brunswick Road, Gloucester Gl1 1JZ.
Telephone: 0845 777 3322
E-mail: information@ecclesiastical.com
Website: www.ecclesiastical.com/

The Ecumenical Council for Corporate Responsibility
PO Box 500, Oxford OX1 1ZL.
Telephone: 01865 245 349
E-mail: info@eccr.org.uk
Website: www.eccr.org.uk

Elim Pentecostal Churches
Elim International Centre, De Walden Road, West Malvern, WR14
4DF.
Telephone: 0845 302 6750
E-mail: info@elimhq.com
Website: www.elim.org.uk

Evangelical Alliance
Whitefield House, 186 Kensington Park Road, London SE11 4BT.
Telephone: 0207 207 2100
E-mail: info@eauk.org
Website: www.eauk.org

Fellowship of Independent Evangelical Churches
39 The Point, Market Harborough, LE16 7QU.
Telephone: 01858 434 540
E-mail: admin@fiec.org.uk
Website: www.fiec.org.uk

Foundation for Sport and the Arts
Walton House, 55 Charnock Road, Walton, Liverpool, L67 1AA.
Telephone: 0151 259 5505
E-mail: contact@thefsa.net
Website: www.thefsa.net

Greek Orthodox Archdiocese of Thyateira and Great Britain
Thyateira House, 5 Craven Hill, London W2 3EN.
Telephone: 0207 723 4787
E-mail: mail@thyateira.org.uk
Website: www.thyateira.org.uk/

Heritage Lottery Fund
7 Holbein Place, London SW1W 8NR.
Telephone: 0207 591 6000
E-mail: enquire@hlf.org.uk
Website: /www.hlf.org.uk

HM Revenue and Customs (HMRC)
Telephone: 0845 010 9000
Website: www.hmrc.gov.uk

Impact Giving UK Trust
PO Box 220, Penrith, CA11 1BH.
Telephone: 01768 594 082
E-mail: info@impactgiving.org.uk
Website: www.impactgiving.org.uk

Independent Examiners Ltd
Sovereign Centre, Poplars, Yapton Lane, Walberton, West Sussex,
BN18 0AS.
Telephone: 01243 555 611
E-mail: solutions@iel.org.uk
Website: www.iel.org.uk

Information Commissioner
Wycliffe House, Water Lane, Wilmslow, Cheshire SK9 5AF.
Telephone: 01625 545 745
Website: www.ico.gov.uk

Inland Revenue – see HM Revenue and Customs

Institute of Chartered Accountants in England and Wales
Chartered Accountants' Hall, Moorgate Place, London EC2R 6EA.
Telephone: 01908 248 250
E-mail: generalenquiries.icaew.co.uk
Website: www.icaew.co.uk

Institute of Chartered Accountants of Ireland
Chartered Accountants House, 47–49 Pearse Street, Dublin 2.
Telephone: 353 1 637 7200
Website: www.icai.ie

Institute of Chartered Accountants of Scotland
CA House, 21 Haymarkets Yards, Edinburgh EH12 5BH.
Telephone: 0131 347 0100
E-mail: enquiries@icas.org.uk
Website: www.icas.org.uk

Institute of Fundraising
Park Place, 12 Lawn Lane, London, SW8 1UD.
Telephone: 0207 840 1000
E-mail: info@institute-of-fundraising.org.uk
Website: www.institute-of-fundraising.org.uk

Kubernesis Partnership [charity accounting consultancy]
36 Acomb Wood Drive, York YO24 2XN.
Telephone: 01904 788 885
E-mail: info@kubernesis.co.uk
Website: www.kubernesis.co.uk

Listed Places of Worship Grant Scheme
PO Box 609, Newport NP10 8QD.
Telephone: 0845 601 5945
E-mail: nptcallcentreuk@liberata.com
Website: www.lpwscheme.org.uk

The Manifold Charitable Trust
Studio Cottage, Windsor Great Park, Windsor, Berkshire, SL4 2HP.
Telephone: 01784 497 787
E-mail: helen.niven@cumberlandlodge.ac.uk
Website: www.ffhb.org.uk

Methodist Church
25 Marylebone Road, London NW1 5JR.
Telephone: 0207 486 5502
E-mail: helpdesk@methodistchurch.org.uk
Website: www.methodist.org.uk

Methodist Insurance plc
4th floor, Lincoln House, Brazenose Street, Manchester M2 5EU.
Telephone: 0845 606 1331
E-mail: enquiries@micmail.com
Website: www.methodist-insurance.co.uk

National Council for Voluntary Organisations
Regent's Wharf, 8 All Saint's Street, London N1 9RL.
Telephone: 0207 713 6161
E-mail: ncvo@ncvo-vol.org.uk
Website: www.ncvo-vol.org.uk

Pegasus Software Ltd [payroll and accounting software]
Orion House, Orion Way, Kettering, Northants, NN15 6PE.
Telephone: 01536 495 000
E-mail: info@pegasus.co.uk
Website: www.pegasus.co.uk

Presbyterian Church in Ireland
Church House, Fisherwick Place, Belfast BT1 6DW.
Telephone: 02890 322 284
E-mail: info@presbyterianireland.org
Website: www.presbyterianireland.org

PRS for Music
Copyright House 29-33 Berners St, London W1T 3AB
Telephone: 0207 306 4801
E-mail: writerquery@prsformusic.com
Website: www.prsformusic.com

Reliance Bank Ltd
23–24 Lovat Lane, London EC3R 8EB.
Telephone: 0207 398 5400
E-mail: info@reliancebankltd.com
Website: www.reliancebankltd.com

Religious Society of Friends (Quakers) in Britain
Friends House, 173–177 Euston Road, London NW1 2BJ.
Telephone: 0207 633 1000
E-mail: enquiries@quaker.org.uk
Website: www.quaker.org.uk

Catholic Bishops' Conference
39 Eccleston Square, London SW1V 1BX.
Telephone: 0207 630 8220
E-mail: lorraine.welch@cbcew.ork.uk
Website: www.catholic-ew.org.uk

Sage (UK) Ltd [payroll and accounting software]
North Park, Newcastle upon Tyne NE13 9AA.
Telephone: 0800 447 777
E-mail: newbusinessadvice@sage.com
Website: www.sage.co.uk

Salvation Army, UK Territorial Headquarters
101 Newington Causeway, London SE1 6BN.
Telephone: 0207 367 4500
E-mail: info@salvationarmy.org.uk
Website: www.salvationarmy.org.uk

The Office of the Scottish Charity Regulator
2nd Floor, Quadrant House, 9 Riverside Drive, Dundee, DD1 4NY.
Telephone: 01382 220 446
E-mail: info@oscr.org.uk
Website: www.oscr.org.uk

Scottish Episcopal Church
21 Grosvenor Crescent, Edinburgh EH12 5EE.
Telephone: 0131 225 6357
E-mail: office@scotland.anglican.org
Website: www.sscotland.anglican.org

Seventh Day Adventist Church
Stanborough Park, Watford WD25 9JZ.
Telephone: 01923 672 251
E-mail: info@adventist.org.uk
Website: www.adventist.org.uk

Stewardship
PO Box 99, Loughton, Essex IG10 3QJ.
Telephone: 0208 502 5600
E-mail: enquiries@stewardship.org.uk
Website: www.stewardship.org.uk

Tax Management for Clergy
PO Box 6621, Grantham NG32 3SX.
Telephone: 01476 539 000
E-mail: enquiries@clergytaxuk.com
Website: www.clergytaxuk.com

United Reformed Church in the United Kingdom
86 Tavistock Place, London WC1H 9RT.
Telephone: 0207 916 2020
E-mail: urc@urc.org.uk
Website: www.urc.org.uk

Index of Subjects

Authorised official (Gift
  Aid) 181
Authorised overdraft 57
Authorised public
  accountants 96
Authorising expenditure 29
Authority to order goods 29
Averaging in insurance 125
Awkward squad 123

BACS 55
Balance sheet 117
Bank charges 46
Bank charges, recording 20
Bank error 52
Bank loan 57
Bank notes in collection 24
Bank notes 207
Bank reconciliation 49
Bank services 42
Bank statements 49
Banking 41
Banking, paying in
  collection 27
Bankruptcy 209
Baptist Church 185
Basket of goods 66
Bells and whistles 39
Bequests 165
Bills of exchange 54
Bills 20
Birds of the air teaching 62
Blank cheques 46
Blessing of assets 110
BMS World Mission 185
Bold type 106
Bookkeeping 83
Books of prime entry 85
Books 85
Bounced cheques 52
Brackets round figures 85

Brought forward 35
Budget control 65
Budget holders 61
Budget management 63
Budgets 61
Buffer in account 47
Building contracts 156
Building contracts 156
Building fund 12
Building insurance 128
Building Regulations 157
Building work 163
Buildings, value of 119
Business activity, defined for
  VAT 184

Calculator 35
Capital endowment funds 11
Capital gains tax 164
Capital of loan 57
Carol singing 134
Carried forward 35
Cash accounting 73
Cash bags 24
Cash books 85
Cash cheques 54
Cash defined 81
Cash, custody of 25
Cash, keeping separate 23
CCAB accounting bodies 95
Central Board of Finance 188
Certainties of trusts 172
Certified accountants 95
Charge cards 47
Charitable donations 192
Charitable expenditure 117
Charitable Incorporated
  Organisation 80
Charity collections 76
Charity examiners 96
Charity law 68

Charity, recording donations
  to 21
Chartered accountants 95
Chartered certified
  accountants 95
Chartered management
  accountants 95
Cheque number 45
Cheques, cashing 25
Cheques, in collection 25
Cheques, issuing 45
Cheques, legal status 54
Children, employment of 145
Chip and pin 48
Choir members fund 77
Choir, paying 21
Christian Aid collection 76
Church defined 78
Church government 63
Church of England 186
Church of Scotland 188
Church plants 78
Church size and accounts 69
Churchwardens' report 99
CIOs 80
CIPFA 95
Closing the books 103
Codicil 166
Coins 207
Coins, in collection 24
Collection analysis form 26
Collection, banking 27
Collection, counting 24
Collection, payments from 25
Commercial information 205
Commonhold 162
Comparative figures 112
Compound interest 59
Computer software 38
Computer system 6
Concepts in accounting 88

Concerts 78
Concerts, knowledge of 22
Conditions in contracts 155
Confidence in 2
Confidentiality 205
Connexional Property
  Committee 188
Consecrated assets 110
Consequential loss 128
Consideration in
  contracts 153
Consistency concept 89
Construction industry tax
  scheme 160
Constructive dismissal 150
Constructive trust 172
Contingencies 91
Contingent work in building
  contract 159
Contra entries 16
Contract of employment 149
Contractor, engagement
  of 156
Contracts 153
Control of funds 75
Correction liquid 16
Cost of generating funds 117
Cost-plus work in building
  contract 159
CPI 66
Credit balances 85
Credit 83
Creditors 120
Crime prevention 130
Crime, discovery of 206
Cross-casting 32
Crossed cheques 54
Current account 41
Current assets 119
Current assets 82
Current cost accounting 90

Index of Bible Quotations, Law Quotations and Court Cases

Cases

Other material